Bunt! ... *he's no homerun hero.*

What happens when a sharp-eyed kid develops such precise bat control that he can bunt a baseball just about anywhere he wants it? He can hop it. Stop it. Even spin a reverse English on it.

What happens is that one of the oldest skills in the game takes on a surprising new life. What happens is insane infielders, angry pitchers, hysterical chanting fans and a surprising breakout into a late season California League pennant race.

The kid's sudden spark gives the "pretty good" Sierra Bears an unpredictable edge in close games. Suddenly they are on a roll towards the climax of the craziest baseball season ever.

Plainly written for young adults who may not read all that much, *Bunt!* is an inspiring tale that will tickle baseball fans of all ages. A wily skipper, a by-the-rules coach, and a team of upward-bound hopefuls and downward-slipping veterans inherit an unknown who comes aboard with nothing more than an amazing junior college batting average.

Bunt! is an unblinking aficionado's delight that captures the feel and smell, the strategy and lore of the game. *Bunt!* is "inside baseball" at its grittiest best.

Bunt!

Enjoy the Read!

Bill B

Also by Bill Baynes

BOOKS:

A Big League Catastrophe

P'2

Old Light and Indifference (Selected Poems)

STORIES:

The Pitch Whisperer

Nunc and Geo

Silky and the Parrot

The Cowbird's Song

Visit www.billbaynes.com for free downloads or for more information about Bill.

Bunt!

Bill Baynes

Bunt!

Copyright © 2012 Bill Baynes

Silverback Sages Publishers LLC
P.O. Box 1408
Abiquiu, New Mexico 87510

For more information about Silvereback Sages or to order e-book or print copies, visit us at: *www.silverbacksages.com*

Text and Cover design: Seventeenth Street Studios, Oakland, CA 94607
Cover photo: © Lane V. Erickson / Shutterstock
Back cover photo: Bill Baynes

Pre-publication Review Printing
Autumn, 2012

ISBN 978-0-9829920-2-9
Library of Congress Control Number: 2012945516

1. Young adult - Fiction. 2. Sports - Fiction. 3. Baseball - Fiction. 4. California League - Fiction. I. Title

SILVERBACK SAGES

Printed in the United States of America

For Donna Duck, my lifetime partner,
who has accepted baseball into her life and into her home
on a daily basis, at least during the season.

CONTENTS

1

I**T'S THE SECOND INNING** when the kid comes up for the first time. He's wearing a uni that's too big for him and has no number on the shirt. He's rolled the cuffs of the trousers. Already undersized, he looks like a little kid playing with the grown-ups.

The Bears have runners at first and third with two outs. The Slammers pitcher has a pretty good move to first and he's paying close attention to Juan, who hit a single up the middle.

From his post in the chalk box by third base, Coach sends a take sign:

Chin ear chin ear chin nose cap nose. Clap, Clap.

The kid looks over and smiles a little and turns his back on Coach. No nod. Nothin'. Coach has no idea if he got the message.

It's a ball, way outside.

Coach doesn't know very much about the rook. He had a flashy batting average. That's why Skip tagged him. He assumes he's a power hitter. That's what the Bears need.

On the next pitch, he relays the Skipper's signal to hit away and try to score Johnnie from third.

Chin ear belt nose chest belt chest chin. Clap, Clap.

The rook turns back to the plate. Coach whistles to get his attention. He wants a nod, something that shows he understands, but he doesn't respond. Coach creeps down the line as close to home as he can get.

The pitch is low and outside. The kid brings his top hand higher on the bat and leans over like he's touching his toes. Then he seems to stumble and he swats at the pitch. It seems almost accidental.

The ball rolls toward third, then bites like a golf ball on a green and jigs unexpectedly to the right.

The third baseman and the catcher go after it. When the ball changes directions, the third baseman clips the catcher in the mouth with his glove. The catcher falls sideways and rolls into the pitcher, Lawry, who collapses on top of the ball.

The third baseman steps back to avoid the pile and puts his hands in the air. There's nothing he can do.

Sporting a wide grin, Johnnie Jett comes in from third with the first run of the game. Coach is windmilling his arm at Juan, who steams all the way from first with the second run.

The kid gets to second, his oversized uni flapping around his legs, before the Slammers pitcher gets his hands on the ball and makes him stop.

The fans are roaring. Both dugouts echo with laughter. The other infielders shake their heads and try to help their teammates back to their feet. Even the catcher, pitcher and third baseman wear silly grins.

Robbie grounds out on the next pitch. The rook is stranded.

"What a freak play," Coach says, coming back to the dugout.

"I've never seen anything like that," Skip agrees.

"Must have hit a hole in the turf," Coach says.

The score is still at 2-0 in the fifth, when the kid comes up for the second time with the bases empty.

The PA announcer gets a little carried away.

"Now batting: number nothing," he intones, referring to the fact the rook's not wearing a number on his shirt. "He got that nothing hit last time up. Let's see what he can do this time."

There's some scattered laughter in the stands and a few boos.

Coach gives the kid another take sign. That means the batter is supposed to stand there and let the ball go by.

Chin ear chin ear chin nose cap nose. Clap, clap.

Lawry has obviously been waiting for a chance to get even. He was embarrassed by the rook's first at-bat. On the first pitch, the big lefthander rears back and sends a screamer right at his head.

The kid looks like he's expecting it. He never ducks back. He slides his top hand up again, putting the bat into a vertical position. As both corner infielders charge the plate, he calmly slaps a ball that was heading right for his face.

It goes directly toward the pitcher's right or pivot foot. Lawry's motion swings his body to the right. The ball caroms off his shoe toward third.

"Owww!"

By the time the catcher can get to it, the rook is standing safely at first.

The pitcher hops around, holding his foot. The stands are in an uproar again, fans pointing and hooting.

Lawry hobbles on both feet for a few moments until the sting goes away. With the trainer looking on, he takes a few practice throws to show he can stay in the game.

The kid dumps the dirt out of his rolled pant legs. He refuses to smile. He doesn't want to show up the pitcher. He won't look at him.

Lawry glowers at the rookie. Clearly upset, he starts to sweat, even though the evening air is getting chilly. He paces around the mound and lingers on the first-base side.

The home plate ump motions for the pitcher to get back to work.

"Let's go. Play ball!"

Lawry climbs onto the mound, puts his foot on the rubber and bends over to get his sign. The kid takes two steps off first and immediately breaks for second, his overlarge shirt billowing behind him.

At his catcher's frantic gestures, Lawry turns back to first and sees that the runner isn't there. He swivels back and slings the ball toward second. The ball skips under the infielder's glove and into center field.

The rook trots over to third, then brushes a dust cloud off his pants.

The pitcher grimaces and picks up the rosin bag, trying to regain his composure. The kid keeps looking down.

Coach is irritated. He leans across the chalk box and whispers into the rook's ear.

"What do you think you're doing? I never gave a steal sign."

The kid flashes a big excited grin at him.

The Bears don't score again and the Slammers hit a two-run homer in the sixth to tie the game.

The kid comes up for the final time in the eighth inning with no one on base. Lawry throws at his feet twice, making the rook skip, and then hits him square in the butt.

The ump ejects the pitcher from the game, as the kid jogs to first. It's his third time on base in three tries.

The Slammers go on to win with a three-run rally in the eighth.

As he comes off the field, it hits him like a falling piano. He's done in, dog-tired, whipped. Three days with no sleep. Bennie squirms on the dugout bench, his rear dented where that pitch got him. He almost drops into a doze as the Bears take their last at-bats.

He comes out of the shower in a daze, wrapping himself in a towel, standing there and spacing. He can hardly keep his eyes open.

"You OK, kid?" asks Pedro, the big bald first baseman.

The kid nods absently. He feels pretty good about the night, but he's really hungry and he's suddenly freezing. He has no clothes except the ones he's already worn for 70 hours and they're in a pile on the tiles because he has no locker. He goes over to Smitty, the equipment manager, the only person he knows.

Before the game, the guys were dragging. It was a long bus ride for them coming in from Grass Valley. They were sitting and staring straight ahead, not interested in welcoming the eager youngster.

Bennie didn't mind it then. It was enough for him to be with the other players. He dressed by himself in the corner of the room. He glanced at the list of signs that Smitty handed him, along with the oversized uniform, socks and spikes.

Now Smitty gives him the only clean clothes he has left, a uniform that's two sizes too small. He advances some cash—turns out that's considered equipment around here—and he explains where the motel is.

"Give 'em this here." He hands him a paper with his signature scrawled on it. He scratches his grizzly gray whiskers.

The mood is not upbeat, not after a Bears loss, but some of the players try to get to know the new kid.

"Nice steal," says Devon, the wiry black shortstop, as they chew on the sandwiches left out for the players.

"Two of the luckiest hits I've ever seen," says Johnnie, the third baseman, piling cold cuts onto a paper plate. He grins at the kid.

All the guys on the team seem old to Bennie. He's never competed against anyone except boys his own age. He feels a little over his head, but that doesn't stop him from gulping down four sandwiches.

"A growin' boy," Devon says.

"Wouldn't think it to look at him, would you?" Johnnie laughs and pats the kid's flat gut.

Bennie grins. He washes down the food with glasses of milk.

He calls a taxi to take him back to the bus station, so he can pick up his belongings. He falls asleep on the ride.

At the motel lobby, he hands over Smitty's paper and hugs his pack.

"Can I see some ID?" the clerk asks.

Bennie fishes out his student card.

"Don't you have a driver's license?"

"Nope. Sorry."

He's never even been inside a motel before. He rubs his eyes, his shirt riding up, while the clerk taps at his computer.

"You don't look old enough to get a room by yourself," the clerk says.

"Made it by three weeks," Bennie says, yawning widely.

He flops onto a big comfortable bed and falls asleep thinking, *only yesterday …*

He was in the middle of the student union, his head on a pile of books next to a littered cafeteria tray. A kid playing pinball pointed him out to the suit.

"Benjamin?"

His answer, muffled in *Masters of Modern Literature*: "Don't call me that."

It was finals week in his freshman year at Skyline Community College. Eighteen-year-old Bennie had been up for the last two nights, cramming for exams. He was exhausted. The suit shook his hand, gave him a Sierra Bears cap and told him to be in Pismo tomorrow.

His tiredness dropped away like taking off a shirt.

He threw everything he owned into one large duffel bag. He was too excited to sleep on the big bus jouncing down the coast. He could hardly sit still. He ground his teeth and glared out the window.

Towering neon signs slipped by in the night. Two hundred seventy slow miles with lots of detours to terminals in warehouse districts, everything closed except vending machines and ugly bathrooms.

All the time, it was running through his mind over and over. This was what he'd been working for his entire life. This was it!

He finally wound down at about 5:30 a.m. and he was ready to rest, but that was when the bus pulled into San Luis Obispo and he staggered stiff-legged and blinking into the pre-dawn cold.

He had only a few dollars and nowhere to go. He assumed the Bears would have a place for him, but he didn't know where they were staying. He didn't care.

He stowed everything in the bus station locker, except for his mitt and his cap. Coffee in a nearby diner and he set out to explore the town. A new place. He'd never been anywhere before. He'd never been off the Peninsula, unless you counted that game against Oakland.

He soon discovered that he was 15 miles from the field. He didn't care about that either. That was an easy walk for him and he'd just as soon be moving. He strolled through the early morning, smiling, squinting into the rising sun. He never thought to hitchhike. There was a bounce in every step.

He followed the Route One along the ocean and then veered east along a road lined with strip malls. It was warmer the farther inland he hiked.

He got there before noon. The big parking lot was empty. The gates were locked. He walked around the perimeter until he got to the outfield. The fence was only about eight feet high at that point and he scaled it easily.

Inside the field was much more spacious than Skyline and had a lot more seats, but it was totally deserted. All the doors were locked, so he couldn't get in anywhere. He was too antsy to wait quietly.

He did a few jumping jacks and some push-ups. He loped around the field a few times and did some stretches. He decided to run the steps in the stands for nearly a half-hour. He worked up a good sweat.

Still no one around. He found a shady spot in the outfield, where he could see the entrances. He slid to a sitting position, one leg stretched in front of him and waited. He couldn't keep a little smile off his face.

Next thing he knew his eyes snapped open and he was looking at an old guy in a Bears cap by the visitor's dugout. He bounced up and trotted over.

"Are you the equipment manager? Can you open the locker room? Do you know where I can get my uniform?"

"I'm Coach Jackson."

"Oh, sorry. I'm Bennie."

And when the name didn't do anything, he added: "The new guy?"
He held out one hand. He was streaky with sweat.

"From Daly City?" Coach asked and the kid nodded happily.

"Bennie Bruno." The hand was still out there and Coach shook it.

"Smitty's your man." Coach pointed toward the guy lugging three huge gray packs, just getting off the bus with the rest of the team.

They're always so eager when they first get here, Coach thought. All capital letters. BIG CHANCE! FIRST DAY! OH, BOY!

"Did you talk to the kid?"

Skip takes a sip of coffee. He and Coach are having breakfast at a local diner.

"I was gonna grab him on the bus back to the motel," Coach says. "but he wasn't on it."

"Maybe he was working out his apology," Skip says, chuckling.

"Ha."

The manager is an optimist. You have to be to run a minor league club.

The other day Van Vranken went off on him about his favorite subject, how he'll never make any money from the Bears, how the team is his curse and he never should have bought it. He had those horrible checkered pants on. It was hard to look at him.

Van said to him in that big basso voice he loves to use: "Skip, how do you stay so calm?"

"I can't help it. It's the way I am," Skip said with a smile as he hefted his widebody off the dugout bench. "Don't worry. They'll start winning."

He squeezed the owner's shoulder and walked away, leaving Van content for the moment.

Skip is good at that. He's deft with people. A Triple-A team is a mixture of different personalities—old vets at the end of their careers, young guys full of energy and hope, a few just playing for paychecks. Skip keeps them all heading in the same direction.

"I don't know whether to laugh or cry," he jokes about Bruno. "The kid did get on base three times."

"Those were flukes," Coach says. "He surprised 'em."

"I'm not sure they were," Skip says. "They told us he has some gimmicks."

There's a nice view of the Pismo Pier out the window, but Coach isn't enjoying it. He's still steamed about last night.

"That kid, he totally ignored me," he says. "He dissed me in front of the whole team. He never even registered my signs. And it's not his decision when to run."

As third base coach, he rules the infield when the Bears are at bat. He's the man the runners have to watch. From first to home, they come into his country. He's the one who says who goes and who stays put.

The batters have to watch him too. He's the one who gives the signals they're supposed to follow. After every pitch, Coach checks with the Skipper and then relays his wishes to the batter and any runners.

Skip slurps some more coffee. He lets Coach stew for a few minutes.

"Baseball is about nine guys playing the same game at the same time," Coach says. "The kid is playing like he's the only one on the field."

"I know. I know. You're right," Skip says, "but those tricks he pulled, they sure tickled the fans."

He promises he'll speak to the kid.

"Not bad for his first game," he says, standing and hooking his thumbs under his belt so he can hike his pants up under his belly. "Pretty entertaining."

"It's not some damn clown show," Coach grumbles. "It's baseball."

The two go a little long, so Coach is a few minutes late for his next appointment, which is a batting session with Bruno. He's also the Bears hitting instructor.

When he gets there, the rook is nowhere to be found.

Coach walks through the clubhouse, but Bruno's not there either. He hangs around for a bit, but the kid doesn't show up.

A few hours later, Coach is back at the park. The first person there, as usual, he's trying to find an edge, something to use, anything. His job is to see everything.

He didn't have time the night before. By the time the Bears got into their uniforms and went through their warm-ups, it was the top of the first. The guys were moving slowly. They had to be herded like puppies.

This is the first series the Bears have played in Pismo Beach this year. The Slammers have made a few changes since last year. They've added two rows of seats behind home plate and one along the basepaths. That means there's less distance to the backstop and less foul territory.

T.J. ran out of room last night when he tried to catch those pop ups behind the plate. But the veteran catcher caught a bounce from that backstop in the fourth inning and threw out a runner trying to take second on a wild pitch.

That big scoreboard was a problem toward the middle of the game. It reflected glary light right behind the pitcher when the sun set. Made it hard for the hitter. The pitcher will have an extra advantage for a couple innings tonight too.

But it's calm. No wind, to speak of. The ball will carry and that's good for the hitters.

The fog won't be a factor tonight. It's too far offshore. But Pismo is cool, typical for a California coastside town. The city, not the team. The Slammers are hot. They're having a great year, leading the Pacific Coast League.

The Bears are not. They suck.

Coach watches the team warm up. He's amped. That's normal for him. He's going a mile a minute. It's how he stays so skinny.

"C'mon, c'mon. Let's go. Look sharp out there." Clap, clap.

Devon still looks stiff, his second game off the disabled list. He's been too hurt to play for nearly three weeks. His range will be smaller at short. Johnnie can cover a little more territory at third to make up for it like he did last night.

Coach is right behind the cage for batting practice. He wouldn't miss BP. As hitting coach, it's his job to make those swings things of beauty. He levers the players to the next level of their ability.

"Keep that head still, Johnnie. Don't try to kill it."

It's just a question of time before Jett is in the Majors. Same with Juan, the number three hitter, the brawny rightfielder. The Bears depend on them both.

"Atta way, Juan. Atta way. You're gonna do some damage tonight."

Coach digs the rhythms of the warmup—the balls coming in and going out, the thwack of the bat and the clip of the glove. Comforting sounds to an old baseball man.

Now Pedro—Coach isn't sure if he'll go much higher. He's got to stop striking out so much and he needs to shed a few pounds. He grunts after he takes a big cut and misses.

"Hey, Pedro. A smaller step. Bat flat. Bat flat."

They know what he's talking about. They've worked together on all these details before in their individual sessions.

Coach learned everything he knows in the Bigs. A .276 average over eleven years. A .420 on-base percentage. There's a lot he's got to teach.

"Let's go! Let's go! You ain't got all day. Let's go!" Clap, clap.

These guys would be late to their own funerals, if he weren't here to hassle them. That's what Coach thinks.

The Slammers are sending their best pitcher to the mound. Charlie Sparks is a gangly kid, all arms and legs. He's got a nasty fastball and a curve to go with it.

As the Bears go back into the clubhouse, Coach stays on the field to see if the young hurler tips his pitches. If he does, Coach can't see it. He times him in the windup and in the stretch. He's got a pretty compact motion. He'll be hard to steal on.

He watches Mattie get ready too. The Bears canny old starter has got all four pitches tonight. He'll be tough to beat. Coach gives him his jacket when he comes over to the dugout.

"Thanks, Coach." He stomps on the top step to get the dirt out of his spikes.

The game gets started to cheers from a crowd of about 60 locals. That's when Coach really goes to work, standing in his box near third. He's constantly active, which suits his personality. He communicates with his hands.

The first pitch: *cap ear cap ear cap chin cap nose.* No meaning, just a lot of hand jive. Clap, clap.

You've always got to clap. That lets them know the sign is over. It lets them know he believes in them. And it helps to keep them alert.

"Way to go. Way to go." Clap, clap.

Coach is talking to the third-base ump, trying to get him to trust him, trying to build a relationship. He's hassling the opposing third baseman. He's talking the boys up, trying to keep them up. He's sending in Skip's signals.

He dances up and down the third baseline from one end of the box to another. He's usually soaking wet by the time a game is over. He gets his exercise, but pays for it next day when he gets up sore. He'll never let the guys know that.

Bruno comes up in the bottom of the second. His uni looks better on him. Smitty must've had time to take it in. And Skip must have talked to the kid because he's real careful to get Coach's signs.

Chin ear chin ear chin nose cap nose. Clap, clap.

Coach gives him the take sign and the kid lets the pitch go by.

Coach gives him another: *Chin ear belt chest belt chest chin cap.* Clap. Clap.

Bruno hits one of those little dippy things and the Slammers third baseman throws him out.

"What was that?" Coach demands him as he passes by the third-base box.

"You said I could hit away," the rook says.

"That's not hitting." Coach tells him.

Skip sees the exchange, but doesn't say anything. When the Bears go back on the field, he pats Coach on the back as he comes back to the dugout.

In the fifth, Bruno comes up in a tie game with the bases loaded and only one out. The Pismo pitcher is in trouble. The Bears want to make him throw as many pitches as they can in hopes that they can force him out of the game. Coach gives the kid the take sign again.

Chin ear chin ear chin nose cap nose. Clap, clap.

Bruno nods and then he chops at the first pitch. He sends a scooter toward first that actually hits the bag and bounces back toward the pitcher, who picks it up and throws him out. The runner scores from third.

After the inning is over, Coach confronts the kid at the dugout steps. He's got his glove on and is headed out to second.

"I told you not to do that. You ignored my sign again."

"Sorry, Coach, but I wanted to get that run in," the rook says.

"You decided that on your own?" Skip jumps on him before Coach gets a chance. "Take a seat, son. Warm some pine. "

He points to the utility infielder, an old guy who can play anywhere.

"Frankie, get out there."

Eight a.m. the following morning, Bennie waits in the cage at home plate, watching the slightly bent older man advance toward him. Coach walks like he's impatient to get wherever he's heading. He carries two bats.

The Bears have a day game, the last one of the set with Pismo. Coach is squeezing in a hitting session.

Bennie feels a little shaky. To get yanked in the middle of a game, that got his attention. No one ever objected before when he batted in a run. It doesn't seem fair to him.

He doesn't know what to expect when Coach comes up to him, standing a little too close.

"Where were you yesterday?"

"I overslept, Coach. Sorry." Bennie moves back a step.

"You been avoiding me?" Coach demands.

"No sir. I didn't get much rest the last couple days. I was catching up."

Coach considers that, holding one bat in each hand.

Bennie puts his arms behind him, bends over and stretches them as high as he can reach.

"You some kinda Ichiro freak?" Ichiro Suzuki, the Seattle superstar, has an elaborate stretching ritual he performs in the on-deck circle.

"Just trying to get loose, Coach."

Coach gives the rook a bat and tells him to step in and swing it. Bennie takes a few half-hearted hacks and looks at the older man.

"I didn't tell you to stop."

He swings some more and Coach doesn't like what he sees. Bennie can tell.

"Coach, I've got a pretty unorthodox style."

"Unorthodox? What is this? Some kinda church? This is professional baseball. This is the Bears."

"Coach, I ... "

"Just do what I tell you and you'll do fine," Coach says. "Let me see that swing again."

The kid takes a few more cuts before Coach stops him. He goes out to the mound and cranks up the pitching machine.

"Now let's see you hit a few."

He stands to the side and watches the kid whack about 20 pitches. There's not much power there. Nothing goes close to the fence. What you'd expect from a smallish guy like Bruno.

But he hits every one of them. He has an eye. Coach will give him that.

The rook's top hand has a tendency to inch up the bat. Coach grabs it and jerks it down the handle, next to his other hand.

"Keep that hand down. Hold the bat tight with both hands."

"But ..."

"Just do what I say."

"I … I … I get better control when I put my hand up higher," Bennie says.

"And you lose all your power. It's not manly. It's dinky. Stop chopping your bat. Swing flat. "

"But …"

"No buts. Stop it right now. Flat through the strike zone."

Bennie tries. It looks awkward.

"Look at your feet. You're standing all wrong."

Bennie doesn't understand. He thought they'd want his special skills. That's how he got that .380 batting average. He looks up and heaves this big sigh.

"This isn't going work for me. I'm not that kind of hitter."

"Not yet," Coach says, "but you're gonna be."

"Coach, I've got a very personal style. I play smallball."

"Not around here you don't. If I tell you to hit a fly ball, I need to know you can do it. If you want to play for the Bears."

That Bennie understands. He definitely doesn't want to go back to Daly City.

Coach loads up the pitching machine again and spends the next half-hour trying to get the kid to hit the ball in the air.

He's not very good at it and he's not a very happy camper. Too bad, Coach thinks, but it's not his job to leave 'em smiling.

A couple days later back in Grass Valley, there's a lot of ribbing going on at BP, a lot of high humor. The boys are pretty loose when Bruno steps in.

"Show me how to hit one o' them there spinners, Junior," Johnnie says.

Bennie looks at Coach, who shakes his head.

He swings flat like Coach taught him, but late. He's still not used to it. He misses the ball.

"Oops. You lost something, kid?" Johnnie comments.

"Yeah," says T.J., the catcher and team captain. "His hits."

"Look under the plate, kid," Johnnie says. "Sometimes they hide under there."

The rook doesn't respond at all to the ribbing. Nobody much likes that.

"Again." Coach says.

The kid swings again, nice and flat. He hits a lame grounder.

"Keep at it." Coach says.

"Keep on keepin' on," Pedro quips in his Spanish accent.

Coach is trying to totally rework the kid's stroke. Bruno wants to bat "at" the ball. Coach wants him to make the bat meet the ball.

Bennie hits a few more foul tips and harmless pop flies. Coach goes back to the clubhouse. He's got things to do to get ready. The rook will get it, he thinks. Eventually.

But Bennie goes hitless for the next two weeks. He never hits the ball hard in the air.

It gets so bad that Skip and Coach talk about throwing the rook back, like some short fish, but they don't have any better options. His sharp defensive play at second keeps him on the team.

BP becomes the Bruno Project. Everybody gathers around the batting cage to watch the kid take his turn. Everybody has advice.

"Keep that head still, Bennie," T.J., the stocky catcher, tells him.

"Try putting your weight on your back foot at first," Juan offers.

"Nah," says Pedro. "Stay up on your toes."

"It's the follow-through," says Carlos, the speedy centerfielder. "Think where you want the ball to go."

The Bears focus on the rook's troubles so they don't have to look at their own. They've lost their last five games.

But Johnnie has another agenda.

When Coach isn't around, he says: "C'mon, kid, give us one of those squibbers."

Bennie does what he's asked. He drops a bunt that kicks up dirt in front of the plate, hops to the left and stops dead.

"How do you do that?" asks Devon.

The kid just grins.

"You can do that on purpose?" Pedro steps in close.

"Do it again," says Johnnie.

He drops one that dies two feet in front of home.

"How 'bout that?" Carlos exclaims.

But there aren't many of those moments. Bennie spends most of his time trying to please Coach, who is usually watching him closely. The kid starts to stroke the ball a little better. He gets a few solid line drives into the outfield and some zip on his ground balls.

"Now you're getting it," T.J. says.

"The kid ought to go back to his small stuff," Johnnie mutters. "Let him do what he knows how to do."

Coach scowls at him. "Brunoburger."

Johnnie throws his hands over his face in mock fear.

"Thatta way, kid," he calls when the rook hits a long fly.

Two wins, eight losses in the last 10 games. Everyone's glum. Everyone's edgy.

"I hate it. I hate it," Devon complains. "I don't want to get up in the morning. I don't want to come to the park at night."

Then Coach has to take a personal leave because his father is sick.

"Just what we need," Skip grumbles, but he's careful not to let Coach overhear because he knows it's not his fault.

The first game he's gone, the Bears play Rancho Cucamonga. The Quakes are a good team and they're playing well. The Bears battle bravely, but it's hard going. After five innings, they're behind 3-2.

Bennie makes the third out, hitting a grounder to short and stranding runners on second and third. Visibly upset, he throws his bat halfway up the third baseline.

Johnnie hands the rook his glove as they go back on defense. He nods toward the dugout, the Skipper by himself at the rail. Coach is usually next to him.

"Strange without the old man here, isn't it?"

Next inning in the dugout, Johnnie is jawing at the kid, his voice real low so Skip won't eavesdrop. Bennie looks straight ahead, but he's listening.

"So what do you want me to do?" Bennie asks.

"Play your game, kid," Johnnie answers. "That's what got you here in the first place."

"I see the way they treat you," Bennie whispers. "You've got nothing to lose. But I do."

"Is that so? Are you sure of that?"

Bennie hits another grounder in the seventh, another out. Johnnie raises his eyebrows at him.

The score remains the same, the Bears down by a run, until the bottom of the ninth, when the Bears mount another attack. Pedro walks and takes second on a passed ball.

The kid goes to the bat rack to get ready to hit after Juan. Johnnie meets him there and hands him a bat.

"You ought to try one of these lighter models," he says. "You can do so much more with 'em."

Bennie takes the bat from him and stands in the on-deck circle as Juan sacrifices Pedro to third.

One out and a runner at third—the perfect situation for a sacrifice fly to the outfield. That's the sign Skip gives the kid.

Cap ear belt nose chest belt chest chin. Clap, Clap.

The kid had behaved all game. He'd followed all the manager's hand signals. Now he never hesitates.

The first pitch is a screamer fastball on the outside part of the plate. He bunts the ball down the first baseline.

The first baseman was playing back, expecting the batter to hit the ball hard. As he charges in, the ball gives a little bounce to the left. The first baseman overruns it entirely.

The pitcher twirls and lunges behind the mound for the ball. By the time, he regains his balance and can throw, Bennie is standing safely on first and Pedro has crossed the plate. The contest is tied.

Three pitches later, Devon slams a long single off the right-field wall. Bennie gets a good jump and runs like crazy. He slides just under the catcher's tag and scores the winning run.

The other Bears run out of the dugout and surround him. Johnnie is the first player to pound him on the back.

B Y T H E T I M E C O A C H gets back from his family leave, the genie is out of the bottle. It's too late for him to regain control over Bruno.

Against Lancaster, Bennie taunts the infielders with his bat, crafting a series of cuts, spins and twists that left the Jethawks confused and angry. He takes them out of their rhythm and the Bears take advantage of it. They sweep the series.

The Bears win two out of three in their next series against the Bakersfield Blaze with Bennie's infield hits critical to the victories.

"He's back to all his bad habits," Coach tells Skip on his first game back, a contest against Lake Elsinore.

"We're back to our winning ways," Skip answers. "Leave it be for now. We'll talk about this later."

At least that's how Johnnie tells it to the guys in the locker room. He says he overheard them.

"Coach wanted to say more, but Skip wasn't havin' any of it," Johnnie says. "He just give 'im that look."

Everybody knows about that look. It would freeze lava. Skip's friendly to everyone, but stern. He doesn't say a whole lot, but he expects people to listen closely to what he does say.

Skip doesn't believe in over-managing. He doesn't feel he needs to control every aspect of a player's game. He allows room for growth, for personality, for mistakes. Whenever he needs to, he asserts his authority. That's where the look comes in.

The Bears go 8-2 in the next 10 games. Bennie keeps the opposing teams off balance with his amazing bat control.

When they play the Varmints, it's 100 degrees at game time. July is a very long month in Visalia. It's the top of the fifth, two out and two on in a 1-1 game when Bennie comes up.

The Varmints played against him in Grass Valley and he made fools of them. They're wise to his apparently impossible dribblers all over the infield. They've developed a special defense.

The third baseman and the first baseman play inside the basepaths. As soon as the pitch is thrown, they both charge the plate. Bennie calmly bloops the ball over the third baseman's head. It rolls into shallow left field and stops, as Bennie pulls up at second with a double.

Both runners score.

On the next at-bat, the Varmints shortstop and the second baseman move toward their right and left respectively. While the two corner infielders charge again, the other two try to guard against another bloop hit. In effect, they're playing a two-level infield against Bennie.

Bennie proceeds to show them what's wrong with that defense. It's based on Bennie's hitting the ball softly, either on the ground or in the air. That's what those spins do. They take the force of the pitched ball and defuse it, minimize it.

But with the sound of rushing feet loud in his ears, Bennie slashes a low liner, a skimmer, down the third baseline. The Varmints third baseman makes a futile stab, but it's by him before he can get his glove down. Behind him, the shortstop simply has no chance. The ball lands 10 feet past the bag and rolls into the corner for another double.

The season is nearly half over and the team is energized. Bennie is the spark. He's winning friends on the squad with his exciting play and he's winning fans.

One Thursday night, the Bears win at home when the opposing pitcher and third baseman crash into each other, trying to field one of Bennie's spinners, and fall to the ground.

More than 200 people are watching and laughing at the slapstick defense. At the end of the game, four local high school girls come onto the field and surround Bennie.

"Hi, Bennie, whatcha doin' later?"

"Bennie, baby, you're so sweet."

"Do you want some cheerleaders, Bennie?"

Bennie is one big blush.

"Uh, do you want some autographs?" he stammers.

They squeal and offer him various body parts to sign. He retreats to the clubhouse.

There's a new spirit there, as well. The guys are beginning to believe in themselves. They're beginning to believe in Bennie too.

They like him, but he doesn't quite fit in. Most of the players don't know what to make of him, he's so young. They're older and rowdier. He isn't a roughhouse. He's not a party guy.

They treat him like a little brother.

"Don't suppose you play cards, do you, kid?" Juan Murillo is host of the Rainout Sweepstakes. He plays poker a lot better than he plays right field, but he's a big bat.

"Sorry, Mr. Murillo," Bennie says. "I never learned."

"It's not too late, kid."

"Don't listen to him, Bennie." Pitcher Abe Emery warns. "He'll take you for every penny you've got."

"Do you guys play for pennies?" Bennie asks innocently.

Johnnie laughs.

Coach feels like he's in the Twilight Zone. He can't get that theme song out of his head: *Neener neener. Neener neener.*

He's the hitting instructor, but he's not supposed to pay any attention to the biggest batting problem on the team—Bruno. The kid can barely hit the ball out of the infield. His stroke is better suited to ping pong.

Yet Bruno goes on a hitting spree. He's swatting these little infield balls, squibbers and bunts and whatnot, but he's getting on base with them.

What planet are we on? *Neener neener.*

It's an illusion. It's just a streak. Right now, the rook is on top of the world, but things will change.

He's been incredibly lucky. He's had balls fall in when he hardly hit them. His goofy game surprises people the first time they see it. Once opposing teams get used to it, once they figure out how to defend him, they'll destroy him.

"He's hitting .450 over the past three weeks," Skip says. "You've got to respect that."

He won't keep it up. He can't. He's a rookie. What does he know? Baseball is about using the whole field to hit the ball. It's about challenges between batters and pitchers, one-on-one. Not trickery. Not some outdoor billiards game.

Coach is the designated bad guy on the Bears, but he's supposed to make nice with the only player on the team who totally disrespects him—Bruno.

Neener neener.

The Bears are in Chico. Hot as Hades. It's like playing in a sauna, even under the lights. The rook comes out for warm-ups with his shirt unbuttoned and hanging out of his pants. He starts to field some grounders.

Coach hot-foots across the infield and tells him to tuck that shirt in.

"C'mon, Coach, give me a break," he whines.

"That don't matter. Button it up. Tuck it in."

"It's roastin' out here, Coach."

"This is not some little league squad, young man. We're professionals and we act like it."

Bruno shakes his head and tucks in the shirt. Coach catches him grinning at Johnnie, who's watching the whole thing with a smirk on his face.

"I'm the Skipper's eyes," Coach says, walking away, wiping the sweat from his face with a big handkerchief, secretly wondering if it's true.

Coach is the manager's confidant, his chief strategist. He thinks Skip should pay attention to his advice. At the same time, he worries that Skip thinks he's lost objectivity about the kid.

He and Skip were friends at school. They played together when they were coming up. Skip was the catcher and Coach played third in Triple A. Then Skip caught that concussion, his fourth in one season, and his Big League career was over before it began.

Eleven years later and Skip's the first one to ring when Coach's back goes out, when his major league career goes out like a match. Coach remembers that lifeline. It made him a lifetime loyalist, but ….

"Micah …," Skip says, when Coach complains about the rook, "you need to get to know him a little. Then he'll listen to you."

"You're siding with a boy, Skip. He's half my age. That make any sense to you? He's got—what?—six weeks of experience in professional ball? And yet you choose him over me."

"It's not him or you, Micah. Don't take it that way."

"It's impossible not to. You're undercutting my authority. I can't do my job. I'm … I'm gonna have to resign."

"Oh, no, don't do that! Please."

"Wouldn't you?"

"Micah, I want to see where the kid's streak goes. I've never seen anything quite like it before, the way he squirrels that ball around. I want to see what happens. You get to do that once in a while in the minors. You get to experiment."

"Be careful it don't blow up in your face."

He's looking around to see if he's slipped into a different dimension. *Neener neener. Neener neener.*

"Whatever you say, Skip," he snorts.

He doesn't know what to do. It's burning him up, all this conflict. His stomach is upset most of the time. The players know he's not happy. Nobody says anything, but when he walks by eyes roll, winks clink like little plastic game pieces.

Coach is pleased that the team is winning, of course, but this is an uphill time for him. Bruno avoids him. He tries not to look at him. He won't schedule another hitting session.

The other guys see it. Devon missed his hitting session Tuesday. He said it wasn't on purpose. He forgot. Coach isn't so sure.

Neener neener. Neener neener.

Johnnie Jett prides himself. At an age when most of his peers are still adrift or just settling into their first real jobs, he's way ahead of the curve. He's on the verge of success.

He's strong and focused. He has a habit of early exercise. It's one of the things that sets him apart from most of his teammates. Besides, he likes that gentle morning light after those banks of superbrights at night games.

He's jogging across Grass Valley, toting his small backpack. He runs from his apartment down side streets to avoid what little traffic there is. Pickups and service vans mostly at this hour, parents dropping their kids at school or daycare. Working people. Bears fans, most of them. He can see the team insignia on the bumpers.

Johnnie likes it here in this small foothill town. The people are friendly. He waves to the guy unloading soft drinks, "Sierra" emblazoned above the bill of his cap. As he cuts across the shopping center parking lot, Johnnie throws a salute to the old guy he sees every day at the vegetable market.

In the three years since he was drafted out of college, he's played on three teams in the minors. A year ago, they called him up to AAA, the Sierra Bears. He's climbing the ladder. It won't be long before he makes it to that final level.

Johnnie is hitting for average (.322), he's batting leadoff and he's one of the team leaders. He thinks of himself as the best man on the team. That's not an ego thing. That's his honest assessment. He thinks he's at the beginning of an impressive career. Formidable baseball—that's what he's all about.

He's a smart hitter. He studies pitchers carefully. He's patient. He murders mistakes.

He's a machine on defense. He's got the fewest errors on the team. He's got a bullet arm. He can nail the fastest runner with a throw across the diamond.

He likes to get dirty. He doesn't feel like he's properly warmed up until his uniform is smudged across the chest and legs. He'd just as soon play baseball on the ground as on his feet.

He doesn't accept that anyone on the Bears is in better condition than he is. That's an important reason why he's playing so well. He's serious about staying in shape. He doesn't stay up as late as most of the guys on the team. Sure, he likes a beer after a game, but he doesn't want to be tired in the morning.

He's feeling pretty good about himself as he arrives at Condon Park. He feels like his life is pretty much on track. He bends over with his hands on his knees and catches his breath. Then he walks for a bit, cooling down, hands on his hips.

Summer mornings. There's nothing like them. Warm. Dappled. The barest breeze. There's a pool here and sometimes Johnnie swims a few laps. Today he takes his racquet out of the backpack and heads toward the courts.

He was going to hit some balls against the backboard, but he'd just as soon play a few games. He's looking around to see if there's anyone who might be interested in a friendly match, when he sees Bruno ambling into the park, carrying a Bears gym bag.

He looks like he's about 14, though Johnnie knows the kid has got to be older than that.

Bruno waves. "Johnnie."

"Hey," Johnnie answers. "Great game last night."

"You really think so?" He honestly seems uncertain.

The kid was on base three times with his little hits. The Bears won by a run.

"You were excellent," Johnnie says.

That brings a smile from the kid. Johnnie bounces a ball on his racquet.

"You play?" he asks.

Bennie is down on his haunches, unzipping his bag. He removes a racquet and looks up.

"Still learning."

It's no contest. Bennie demolishes Johnnie. He humbles him. Johnnie loses a game on occasion, of course. Everyone does. But he isn't used to being manhandled. Very gently and very politely, but manhandled just the same.

Johnnie has a good serve. It's the best part of his game. He uses it to get to no man's land in the middle of the court, where he stands and defends. He uses his speed and agility to get to his opponent's returns. He's skilled at the net, intimidating most challengers with expertly placed slams.

Bennie is unfazed. He puts hard cuts on Johnnie's hardest serves. He has no trouble getting to them. He moves up close on the slams, deftly putting vicious spins on returns that just clear the net and bounce backward into it.

"How do you do that?" Johnnie complains.

The kid grins. He's all over the court. He's always right where Johnnie hits the ball.

But that isn't the worst of it. His serves. Johnnie is stupefied. And he looks it.

Bennie hits balls that float over the net and Johnnie has no clue what direction they'll bounce. He moves up and lurches left, only to have the ball hop right. When Bennie has him off-balance, edging up, he sends a straight serve speeding past him.

Johnnie is breathless in a very few minutes.

"You have a unique style, Bruno. Really. How did you develop it?"

"Bennie. Call me Bennie. Please."

"Well … Bennie, how'd you do it?"

"Playing ping-pong."

They both have a laugh at that.

After a couple sets, Bennie excuses himself. He has this routine before each game to get ready and it takes a while.

"Mind if I tag along?"

As Bennie hooks on his backpack and starts to trot, Johnnie falls into step. There's no question about his keeping up. No question at all. Johnnie's a jock. He prides himself.

After an easy half-mile, Bennie stops at another small park. He takes a jump rope out of his pack and does a quick hundred. While Johnnie takes his turn, Bennie takes out a long rope and stretches it along the sidewalk. He proceeds to demonstrate a series of footwork drills, running the length of the rope frontward and backwards, crossing and uncrossing his legs.

"Agility," he explains.

They go back to the Bears clubhouse and watch videos, munching on fruit and yogurt. They study the pitcher they face tonight and how he threw in his last few starts, how they batted against him in earlier games. They look at the batters they play against tonight, how they swing and where they hit the ball.

They talk about what they see.

"Ooh, that guy's got a nasty curve."

"Yeah, but sometimes he hangs one. If you can wait for that …."

Bennie stretches—long and luxuriously. He hangs by his hands from a chinning bar. He performs tai-chi exercises.

"It's all about balance," Bennie says. "Getting comfortable in your body."

Johnnie follows along, grinning.

Bennie goes outside for what he calls his warm-ups, which are enough to put most people in traction.

Van Vranken Stadium consists of wooden seats for about 500 fans arranged behind home plate and on either side of the field. There's a shuttered broadcast booth at the top of the seats behind home.

The outfield fence butts against a par-three golf course. Golf balls occasionally fall into the field of play during day games and sometimes baseballs roll onto the putting greens.

Bennie runs the seats, about 20 rows to the top, up and down until he finishes 1,000 steps.

Then 100 pushups.

Then he takes 1,000 swings of the bat.

"I like to be a little tired during the game," he says. "Otherwise, I get jittery."

It's hard to smile when you can barely breathe. Bent over, panting, Johnnie looks up and nods.

Next Bennie goes to the clubhouse wall. As other players begin to arrive, he tosses a ball against the concrete and fields the bounces. Five hundred throws. He bends and stoops and scoots from side to side. He gets into a rhythm, a meditative movement.

Johnnie leans against the wall and watches for a while and then he goes into the shower.

The clubhouse is noisy when Bennie finally comes in. The other players are joking and laughing. Bennie is quiet as he dresses and goes onto the field by himself.

He sits against the outfield fence. He pounds the pocket of his glove. He goes over the opposing players in his mind one more time, one by one.

As the other Bears come onto the field, Bennie takes part in the normal team warm-ups—batting and infield practice.

"Where's Jett?" T.J. wonders.

"I saw him on the trainer's table," Devon says. "Flat on his back, taking a snooze."

Middle of July, the Bears are doing great and it's not just Bennie. Johnnie and Pedro, the one and two batters, are both hot. Johnnie is tearing up the league with a .400 average for the last two weeks.

The Bears seem to be having fun. Winning will do that for you. Influenced by Bennie's success, some embrace the smallball concept.

At first, it's good for the team. The players start trying to hit singles, instead of always swinging for the fences. Pedro stops striking out so much. Batting averages rise.

It's hard not to get caught up in the excitement, the gathering momentum, but Coach manages to restrain himself. It's his job to stay objective, to cast a critical eye on everything. He finds plenty of things to complain about.

About the rook. He's still stung that the rook ignored his hitting instructions. He's convinced that Bruno has people fooled. He keeps finding fault. Take Bruno in the field, for example …

The Bears play the Modesto Nuts for the league lead, a home game. For the first four innings, it's a classic pitchers duel. One single for the Bears. A walk for the Nuts. It's scoreless.

The Nuts open the top of the fifth with a drive into right that rolls into the hole between the outfielders all the way to the fence. It takes a good throw from Pedro to hold the Nuts runner at second.

On the first pitch to Bankhead, the next batter, Bruno charges down the first base line. He apparently expects the batter to bunt and he wants to make a play on the runner going to third.

Bankhead takes a gigantic cut, trying with all his might to put a 200-mile-per-hour liner into Bruno's teeth, but he barely gets a piece of the ball. It dribbles in front of the plate. Bruno flops onto his stomach and picks it up. Coach is in his chalk box, shouting, "First! First!"

But the rook bounces to his feet and throws to third. Johnnie, surprised, misses the catch. The Modesto runner rounds third and continues home with what turns out to be the only run of the game.

Inexcusable. In the first place, charging the bunt is a first baseman's role, not the second baseman's. Bruno is out of position. In the second place, the rook should throw to first, like Coach told him. He should always get the safe out. Instead, he causes an error.

When the inning is over, Coach lights into the kid.

"You think this is the Bruno Family Circus or what?" he shouts so everyone can hear.

The front of Bruno's shirt is covered with mud. "Coach, I ... I thought ..."

"Sit down. Shut up."

Bruno has the good sense to do what he's told. Skip just raises his eyebrow like he does.

The rook is overplaying his position. He's showboating. Why doesn't Skip say anything to him?

Bruno on the basepaths ...

There's one out when the rook comes up against the High Desert Mavericks. Playing at the barren ballpark out in the Mojave north of L.A., the Bears are down a run in the ninth.

Bruno has fouled out twice and grounded out in his first three times up. Now Pikonis, the Mavericks closer, is on the mound and he's totally on his game.

Chin ear chin ear chin nose cap nose. Clap, Clap.

Coach gives Bruno the take sign. He wants him to wait a couple pitches until the Pikonis is worried about the count. He's more likely to get a good pitch to hit.

Bruno nods and takes a ball. In fact, he never takes his bat off his shoulder and he manages to get to first on a walk.

Carlos hits a lazy fly to left for out number two. Bruno moves a few feet toward second and then walks back toward first when the ball is caught. The normal thing to do.

The throw goes back toward Draper, the High Desert shortstop, who is deep in the hole, his back to the plate. Suddenly Bruno tags and takes off toward second. Draper doesn't know Bruno is running. There's a crowd gasp and the Mavericks third baseman shouts, "He's goin'! He's goin'!"

Draper glances back and, in that instant, he takes his eye off the ball. When the throw arrives, he juggles it before he throws to second. Too late. Bruno is in there, sliding headfirst, his hand reaching the bag.

The crowd is excited. Skip shakes his head. Coach is furious. His mouth is open in disbelief and he's holding his hand to his throat like he wants to choke himself. The steal sign was *not* on. The game is on the line and the rook takes this ridiculous gamble.

Pikonis is mad too. He gets the rosin bag and shakes it over his throwing hand and then hurls it to the ground. He walks around the hill, glaring at Bruno, who is edging off second.

The crowd is loud as leftfielder Winston Rizzo stands in. Acquired after he was released from Bakersfield, he's got a great arm but a weak bat.

Pikonis climbs back onto the mound and makes a big deal about checking Bruno several times before he throws a ball that goes in the dirt. It gets away from the catcher and Bruno advances to third. The rook has this uncanny good luck.

On his next pitch, Pikonis lays one right over the plate. Winston puts a perfect stroke on the ball, the one he and Coach have worked on for hours. He sends it to Tahoe. Game over. Bears win.

A huge victory for the Bears, but a lucky one. Bruno almost lost it. You can't make too much noise when the team pulls out a win, but Coach is still aggravated.

This isn't how a team works together. Good teams have good coaches and the players do what they're told to do. They pay attention to the signs.

"Does he think I'm over there fidgetin' with my hands all the time for no reason? Does he think I enjoy it? That I'm doin' it for my health?"

"Micah, restrain yourself," the manager says when Coach unloads on him. "He's putting fans in the seats. Van Vranken likes that."

Coach hates that reason. "What's that got to do with baseball?" he retorts.

Skip gives him the look. "Micah, you're a vital part of this team. Everybody knows that."

All this is spoiling Coach's supper. He always ate with the guys before when the team was on the road. They came to his table so they could talk baseball. These days nobody wants to eat with him any more.

He's not hungry most of the time anyway.

Johnnie and Bennie become tennis buddies. They meet most mornings when there's a night game and run around the court for an hour.

This is a different kind of relationship for Bennie. He hasn't had many friends. Ken was always a little distant, a little top-of-the-hill toward Bennie. Johnnie is intense. He's a headlong kind of guy. He doesn't let up. He throws himself into whatever he does.

If Johnnie Jett respects you, he'll give you anything. He respects Bennie and he's ready to unload his entire bag of tricks for his new friend. His insights into the Bears, who's who and what's what. His secrets for playing third and for getting on base. His favorite haunts and jaunts.

Bennie is slow to know. He holds back. It's almost as if he doesn't want to get too close to anyone.

There are times when it would be real easy to grab a cup of coffee or a smoothie, but he always has somewhere else to go. There are moments when they're taking a rest when it would be real easy for the conversation to get a little personal.

"I hear you're from Daly City," Johnnie would say.

"Yeah. A dump."

And that would be that. Bennie likes to talk, but not about personal stuff. He chatters on about baseball or tennis.

He has no interest in personalities. He's into strategy. He likes to discuss the philosophy of sport. How the game is played. How it can be improved.

Bennie is one of the most serious people Johnnie has ever known. He decides Bennie needs to work on his laughter, that he needs to learn more about having fun.

He convinces Bennie to go the movies a few times.

He introduces him to camping. They go to Scotts Flat in Nevada City and find a site right on the lake. Bennie totally enjoys it, especially the fly-fishing. He's fascinated by the precision of casting the slender rod, the meditative repetition, finding the touch.

One night at supper, Bennie opens up about Coach.

"He's on me all the time. Every day," he complains to his teammate. "The way I hit, the way I run …. He's all bent because I don't pay any attention to him over there at third waving his arms around.

"I'm just trying to protect my game. That old man wants me to drop it. He wants me to stop doin' everything I do."

"You can't let him do that," Johnnie says. "What does Skip think? He's the one who makes the calls. Coach just relays them."

"I don't know. He hasn't said anything to me."

"If he didn't like what you're doing, you'd know it," Johnnie says. "Remember that time he yanked you out of the game?"

"I do. I definitely remember."

After a couple more bites, Johnnie puts his fork down.

"Truth is, I talked to Skip about you. I told him the way you play is a turn-on for the rest of us."

"What did he say?"

"Thanks for letting me know what you think," Johnnie laughed.

"I don't know what I think about you doing that."

"Skip keeps his door open," Johnnie says.

"Well, thanks," Bennie smiles, "I guess."

On a day off, they drive down to Sacramento because Bennie wants to see a magic show. Not a big stage show, where the magician disappears birds or saws his assistant in half. No, this is a close-up performance, a strangely intimate experience. About a dozen spectators perch in a horseshoe of seats, looking down on a felt-covered table, flooded in light. The magician sits inches from his audience.

The Amazing Whatever (Johnnie can't remember) lives up to his billing. He rolls up his sleeves and proceeds to disappear and re-appear coins and cards in front of the spectators' eyes. The things he does seem impossible, but he does them anyway and Johnnie can't tell how.

Afterwards, the two young men walk the tree-lined streets in search of a coffee shop. Nothing is open, but it's a pleasant night.

"Do you know how he does it?"

"It's all in the muscles of his hand," Bennie says. "He's developed these tiny muscles that we don't normally use. At the base of his fingers, for example, or the middle of his palm. He uses them to move cards or coins to either side of his hand or up his sleeve."

"Sounds like tedious work."

"It is. It takes thousands of hours."

"You've studied this, haven't you?"

"A little," Bennie admits.

"Why don't we see it when he moves those things?"

"Two reasons. First, he does it very fast. Second, he misdirects us. He makes us watch something else, usually the wrong hand. You notice that his hands are always moving?"

"The hand is quicker than the eye, I guess."

They walk a little further, basking in the warm air.

"Why did you get interested in magic?"

"I play baseball," Bennie says with a serious expression. Then he breaks into a big grin.

Johnnie realizes it's true. Magic is part of Bennie's game. Feints. Deception. Misdirection. He brings it all to baseball.

Heady days. The Bears are really roaring. Bennie is becoming a force.

The team goes on an extended run. They win with big hits. They win with lucky drops. They win with different heroes every game. They win they win they win.

Twenty straight games.

Bennie is the inspired and the inspiration. The Bears' most consistent player, the fan favorite, his astounding infield work on both offense and defense has people talking about a Player of the Year Award.

The Bears PA announcer, Cubby Burnside, becomes Bennie's amplified advocate. He plays him up because that's what the fans want. He really lays it on thick at times.

"So here comes Bennie Bruno, folks," he calls over the big speakers. "What will he do this time, people? And what will those poor guys on defense do about it?"

Laughter and catcalls from the fans.

"What d'ya say, folks? Let's have a little B-ball. How about it?"

The fans respond with cheers and applause.

"B as in Bears."

Applause.

The crowd shouts: "B!!"

"B as in baseball."

The crowd answers: "B!!"

The crowd is happy. A happy crowd makes a happy owner. Van Vranken beams at the fan response.

"B as in Bruno."

"B!!" screams the crowd.

The announcer hollers: "B as in Bennie!"

The fans roar their approval. Sure enough, Bennie spins a single just inside the first-base line.

"There we go! That's it—that's Bennie Ball, folks!"

They stand and applaud until their arms are sore. They love it.

The name sticks. Everyone picks it up. Van Vranken starts selling hats imprinted with it. Bennie Ball is walking all over town.

Bennie Ball becomes the way the Bears play baseball. It's an attitude, a mindset. An intense, enthusiastic immersion in the game.

The crowds grow. The team does too. In confidence. In expectations. It's a rich brew in those days, seasoned with lots of laughter, lots of winning ways.

Bennie is becoming nearly impossible to stop. It seems like he can get on base almost any time he wants. He's moving up in the batting order. Skip wants to get him more times at bat.

Most teams use some sort of Bennie Ball defense. They move the fielders around to try to make it more difficult for Bruno to get on base. Some even bring one of their outfielders into the infield, creating a three-tier defense: two outfielders, three middle fielders and two infielders inside the basepaths.

It feels more like a life-sized pinball game than regular baseball. Precise, patient, Bennie puts the ball exactly where he wants. Through the legs. Off the shin. Squibs and jibs. Bounces, caroms, anything unpredictable so the fielders don't know what to do.

With all that back and forth, all the extra ground to cover, the infielders get fried. When they're tired, usually in the late innings, they make mistakes on routine balls. That's when the Bears get the lucky breaks, the breaks that Bennie builds.

The Bears begin making noise when they get on base.

"Hup, hup. Hup, hup. Careful, Pitch. Watch out, Pitch. Hup, hup."

This drives opposing infielders crazy.

"You jerks! You babies," they complain.

But the Bears keep doing it. They can see it's making them mad. It's another small aspect of the game. Bennie Ball.

"Careful, Pitch. Watch it. Watch it."

They steal signs from the infielders, when they can, and then they talk about them on the field.

"Hey, Devon. Shortstop covering on the bunt," Juan calls from first base to his teammate on second.

"Look behind you," Johnnie yells from third. "Second baseman creepin."

Baseball is fun for the Bears and for their fans. Through it all, Bennie Ball evolves.

In a game against the Blaze, the pitcher throws him an outside pitch. Bennie brings his bat up and chops it like an axe. The ball slams straight down and bounces really high. The catcher, the pitcher and the first baseman all stand around waiting for it to come down. When it does, Bennie is standing on first.

"We'll call that one the Big Bounce. What d'ya say?" the PA announcer blares.

The fans cheer and laugh.

Burnside names more of Bennie's twisty hits. He creates a Bennie Ball catalog:

- The Gripper, a bunt toward short that bends back toward third;
- The Slipper, a bunt toward the mound that bends back toward first;
- The Tipper, a straight hard grounder that hits first or third, usually causing the ball to bounce up or in different directions;
- The Backup, a top-spun bunt that bites and jumps backwards; and
- The Popover, a bloop fly designed to get over the head of a charging infielder.

Fans savor Bennie's special menu. They argue about which is the most effective twisty. The local coffeehouses, the local buses, the local newsstands—they're all full of people talking about the same thing, Bennie Ball. The Bears are the toast of Grass Valley.

All through July, the team is hot. They have the other teams out-of-synch, a step late, a smidgen sideways. The guys are getting cocky. They have a seven-game lead with 25 games to go in the regular season. It looks good.

But under it all, there's discord on the Bears. It bubbles like a bad meal in an upset stomach.

In the mouth of Coach Jackson. He's convinced the team is heading for a fall. Baseball always evens things out.

He doesn't change his mind. He doesn't go away. He keeps watching, waiting for an opening. He keeps talking to Skip.

"It's not the right way."

"They're all fired up," Skip responds.

"It won't last. It's not the right way."

"The right way is to win."

3

H E DOESN'T REMEMBER much. He was too little.

He remembers being carried. By? It's a man. He remembers the smell of the coat and the sweat. Is that Daddy?

He remembers waking up and there are more smells, many more smells, and the man puts a hand on his chin and turns his head.

Then green. Green green green under bright bright lights.

And tiny men running around down there.

And a feeling of swelling or breathing. So many people and such a sound. A sound that gets bigger and bigger and rests and gets bigger and bigger, growing and growing ....

A green sound ... a growing sound ....

He starts to cry.

"Baseball, Bennie," the man bounces him up and down. "This is baseball. Don't be scared."

Another night. Another stadium. Now he knows where he is. He can follow what's happening.

It's happening very slowly. The ball is heading toward him, the batter just finishing his follow-through in the background. He can hear the crowd noise suspend.

He holds his breath. The ball keeps coming like a big egg dropping from the sky.

He stands. Everyone around him stands.

The ball lands behind him, a few rows back. He twists to watch.

It hits fingers and there is an "Ouch!" and the fingers pull back and the crowd says "Ohhh!" in a drawn-out splash of sound and the ball disappears and then bounces up over a seat toward him.

And other hands try to grab it—two, then three, then six, they're everywhere, blocking what's going on—and the ball slides down the back of a seat into the crushed paper cups and food wrappers and he reaches down and …

and the ball is in his hand.

And the man next to him—Is that Daddy? Is that him again?—holds his arm high, the ball in his hand like a glowing light, like the most important thing in the universe.

He's got a ball, a real Big League ball!

And he pumps his arm and the crowd applauds and it's for him. It's for him! It's for Bennie!

An infant in diapers trips over a sleeping dog on the bottom row. The woman beside him casually reaches over, lifts him up and wipes his nose. A guy reaches into the ice chest on the seat and brings out a soft drink. Two teen boys punch each other's arms.

Wednesday evening and the bleachers are half-full. Most of the parents, brothers and sisters are half-conscious of the action on the field.

Two co-ed squads are playing baseball. The Daly City Deli Dodgers in white on the field and the Broadmoor Plumbing Pirates in gray at bat. Team members are 10 years old, give or take. Some never played before. Most are afraid of the ball.

Not Bennie.

It's his first game, but you'd never know it. While everyone else waits, he does a couple deep-knee bends. He stretches his arms over his head.

It's the bottom of the ninth in a tie game, 18-18. Most people at J.T. Axelrod Park, players and spectators, are ready for this one to be over. The Pirates manager is yawning.

The pitcher is unconcerned. She tosses the ball a couple feet into the air and catches it, underhands it up again and catches it.

Bennie advances to the batter's box like it's mined and he'll explode if he puts his feet in the wrong spot. He places each foot carefully, then leans forward onto his toes, his knees bent in an exaggerated stance.

Most of the kids just lay the bat on their shoulders and stand as far away from the plate as they can. Bennie holds the bat two inches off his shoulder, waggling the tip.

He swings at the first pitch and misses it entirely. The second pitch is high, but he whales at it anyway. The ball bounces once near second and skips into the outfield.

Bennie takes off at full speed. He rounds first as the outfielder bends down and lets the ball scoot between her legs. As she reaches the ball, Bennie is touching second base.

The ball comes back in to the shortstop, who slows it but doesn't catch it. As Bennie comes around third, it caroms to the pitcher, who picks up the ball and throws to home.

The catcher is a girl with long blonde hair in a ponytail. The ball comes in on a bounce. She traps it with her oversized mitt just as Bennie slides into her. She falls backward, bumps her head and drops the ball.

Broadmoor wins! Bennie scores the winning run.

A few cheers as the players run off the field and the folks behind the mesh come to their feet. The catcher is sitting in the dust and sobbing, rubbing the back of her head. Bennie picks up the ball and hands it to her.

"Didn't mean to hurt you," he says.

Ma is all smiles, as she and Mike walk across the field.

"That was wonderful, Bennie," she says. "You won the game."

"Lucky the other team couldn't field," Mike says.

Mike had moved in with them three months ago. A slender Filipino man in a blue warm-up suit, he gets into it with Ma on the ride back to the apartment. Something about what they're going to do later. They start hollering at each other.

"Who's going to watch Bennie?" Ma asks, putting her arm around her son.

"Sarah Ann can do it."

"That's not fair. She's too young to be responsible."

"She's 12. That's plenty old enough," Mike answers.

The hassle continues when they get home. Bennie makes a bee-line for his room, where Sarah Ann is sitting on her bed, talking on her cell. She grimaces at the commotion.

"Shut the door," she says and seeing the expression on her little brother's face, she adds: "Just tune 'em out, Beanie."

Bennie plunks down on his bed and puts his nose in a comic book.

"How'd you do, Beanie?" his sister asks.

"Good. I got a homer."

Ma pokes her head in the door, an apologetic expression on her face. Mike is cursing in the background. Ma looks up at the ceiling. *What can I do? You know how he is.*

"We're gonna go out for a little bit."

Sarah Ann nods. Bennie doesn't look up until the front door slams.

"I'm goin' out too."

"Stay close," his sister says, texting, not looking up. "And put your jacket on. It's foggy."

Bennie takes his gear and goes out back to the Bayshore Village parking lot. Standing in the narrow aisle between 30 parked cars and pickups, still in full uniform, he twirls a baseball in his hand. He throws it up and catches it a few times. He throws it higher and has to run a few steps to catch it with his glove.

Under his breath, he does the play-by-play: "Bruno is under it in deep center. He puts it away."

He throws it higher still and has to lean over a car to catch it.

"A spectacular save. The fans go wild!" he opens his mouth wide and exhales the crowd noise.

"Haahhhhh!"

He's startled by the small beep as a car creeps by him.

Bennie tosses the ball really high and he can't reach it as it clanks off the roof of a parked Toyota. He catches it on the second bounce.

"Hey, you kid, you," calls an old Chinese man, leaning over his fourth-story porch. "Better not break nothing."

Bennie is running through the neighborhood, his teeth bared in something like a smile. It's impossible to sulk when you're moving so fast.

He's wearing shorts, a t-shirt, sneakers and his Giants cap. Plus, of course, that undersized, shapeless kid's glove he's had since Little League. It's all he's got, but he's always got it, flopping against his leg. A ball bulges in his back pocket.

Every few steps he leaps forward, trying to clear a crack in the cement. Sometimes he jumps as high as he can just … for no particular reason. Exuberance.

To see him you'd think he hasn't a worry in the world. But the little apartment is a good place not to be. There was another shouting match after lunch. Bennie shut the door on the sound of a slap and his mother's screech.

Now his running causes the old Chinese man to turn sideways and shield his Starbucks cup with his hand. A stout young woman moves her stroller to the inside of the sidewalk. The boy leaps and spins around.

"Hey, Mrs. Martinez."

"Hey, Bennie."

Bennie goes down Schwerin, past the cramped concrete houses with their tiny yards, past his old elementary school. He hasn't been there since he finished fourth grade the year before and moved on to Bayshore Intermediate a few blocks away.

He passes the chain-link fence around the brick PG&E substation with its sprawling antenna farm. He knows he can't get in there. They won't let kids anywhere near the 80-foot towers that crackle and thrum with electricity for San Francisco and Peninsula cities. There are more than 50 of them. It's like living next to a gigantic metallic forest.

Along Geneva Avenue, three lanes in both directions full of traffic, Bennie slows to a walk down Fast Food Alley—McDees,

Taco Bell, Soul Kitchen, Pizza Palace. He waves to a kid coming out of the Hawaiian Barbeque.

He's looking around, searching for something. He checks out the parking lots, especially the areas away from the street, but that's where the employees normally park.

He pauses by a billboard that towers over gas pumps. He takes a green tennis ball from his back pocket, heaves it against the gigantic picture of a child eating cereal and then fields the rebound like a fly ball, basket-style.

He stops at a pocket park, a small green space the size of three or four lots. It contains a couple picnic benches on tended lawn and a single tennis court backed against a practice wall. The only thing taller than three feet in the park, the nine-foot-high wall was built for players to work on their strokes and reactions.

Bennie goes into a full windup and throws his ball against the wall, but the net across the court interferes with his fielding. If he plays in front of the net, he's too close to the wall to get a good throw. If he stays on the other side of the net, the ball never gets to him.

Off he goes again, hunting for a place he can play catch by himself.

He comes to a 7-11 on a corner and finally finds what he's looking for: a broad empty wall on the side of a building, facing a side street. He tosses the ball against the wall a couple times and catches the bounce back.

Bennie takes a position down the narrow side street, between the cars parked on both sides. He goes into his windup and hurls the ball at the wall. He finishes in his defensive position, ready to field the return.

But the ball comes off the wall sideways and squirts into the intersection. An old VW bus swerves, but can't avoid the ball. It disappears under the right front tire. *Pop!*

Bennie retrieves the ball and sees that it's ruined. Unusable. This wall is, too.

It's getting chilly as the fog creeps in. Bennie wraps his arms around his skinny chest, still wearing that silly glove. He hurries back down Schwerin.

Final bell. The kids thunder out of their rooms and into the yard, laughing and talking and shoving. Bennie, hard to see because he isn't very tall, is the only one standing still.

He leans against the mesh fence, idly twirling another tennis ball in his hand. In a few minutes, he's the last one on the asphalt between the school and a small outlying building, the library. An afternoon breeze pushes some candy wrappers across the open space.

Bennie takes his place about 40 feet from the side wall of the library. He winds up awkwardly and looses the greenish ball at the chipped pinkish concrete. The ball bounces left and he has to dodge the pole of a basketball backboard to get to it.

He sets up and throws again, this time easily catching the ball on one bounce.

He thinks of Mike, slapping his mother. He throws the ball.

He thinks of Dad, who called and said he's sorry but but but. He throws the ball.

He throws the ball again.

Up the hill behind the playground, Ray is busy tending the small school garden. He's a bearded white man wearing a checkered do-rag, the Bayshore janitor. He's a gentle man, a wounded vet, who lives on the edge of the campus in a trailer provided by the school.

He doesn't hear the balls hitting the building right away, but the rhythmic impacts finally register. He looks up from his work, brushes dirt from his knees, and limps a few yards so he can see around the library.

There's Bennie. He's throwing the ball like his life depended on it, like the wall is his enemy.

Ray stands and watches. The boy never notices.

A different day. The sun is bright against the building, the air still.

Bennie throws the ball against the library wall. *Thump.*

He gets to the ball, but muffs the catch. He's not very good, but he is determined. He chases the ball back to the school fence.

He throws the ball. *Thump.*

He catches the ball. He scribbles something on a sheet of paper.

He throws the ball. *Thump.*

He has to chase it again, dodging around the backboard pole. He writes something on his paper.

The ball. The wall. The ball. The wall. The minutes fly by.

Inside the school at a window overlooking the yard stand three adults, watching.

Norm, the principal, is overwrought and overweight. He has a kindly face.

"What's he doing?" he asks.

"Just pitch and catch," replies Vera, the sixth-grade teacher. They're in her room. "Over and over. He's out there all by himself."

"He seems to be keeping score." Susan Robertson, the PE teacher, is a short woman with curly hair and a whistle around her neck. "It looks like he's playing against himself."

"He's out there almost every day," Vera says. She's a long-timer, a kid-lover, a kid favorite.

Bennie throws pitch after pitch. He scribbles. The adults observe.

"He doesn't have any friends," Susan says.

"He's not doing very well," Norm says. "His grades are falling."

"He seems smart enough, but he's distracted," Vera says. "He fell asleep in my class two days ago."

"Maybe some family issues," Norm muses.

"He doesn't seem to care about anything except throwing that ball," Susan says.

"I wish I had more students who cared as much about anything," Vera says.

Murmurs of approval.

Outside, Bennie is still at it, hammering the wall—*thump*—fielding the ball. It's hard to see in the fading light. The boy misses a bounce and has to chase the ball again.

Ray limps down the hill. He's wearing an old first-baseman's glove. He stands at the edge of the yard until Bennie notices him.

Ray pats the pocket of his glove and then holds it up.

Without hesitation, Bennie tosses him the ball.

Ray skids a throw past the boy. "I'm a little rusty," he says.

"It's OK," Bennie answers, a little out of breath.

A couple days later, a Saturday, the boy climbs the hill behind the school and walks past the garden to the custodian's trailer. He sees a man sitting with his back to him on a bench of a picnic table, but he's not sure it's the same guy who played catch with him. He stops and studies the scene.

The table is loaded with lots of stuff—concrete blocks, small plants, small pots, a coil of hose, tools, garden gloves. Bennie notices a cat sleeping on a stack of magazines.

The man has flowing gray hair to his shoulders, but he's bald on top. The janitor always wore that checkered kerchief. Maybe he had a ponytail. Bennie can't remember. The custodian always wears stained blue coveralls, but the guy on the bench is wearing shorts and his legs are tanned.

The man doesn't hear the boy come up, but when the cat jumps off the table he turns around to see why.

"Uh … hello. I didn't know you were there."

The boy doesn't say anything. He looks frightened.

"My name is Ray and this is where I live. You knew that, right?"

"I didn't know your name was Ray."

"What's your name?"

"Bennie. I'm Bennie."

"Whatcha got there?" He points at the glove and ball.

The boy smiles tensely. "I thought maybe …."

"Let me get my mitt."

The rainy season sets in. Short soggy days. School and twilight. Streetlights are on when he gets home.

Sarah Ann is already there, multi-tasking in their bedroom. She's stuffing her face with a Big Mac, listening to her iPod, talking on the phone and watching a sitcom all at the same time. She swats at Bennie when he snatches a French fry.

"Touch any of my shit and you will truly and deeply die," she says pleasantly, her mouth crammed.

Sarah Ann is not his best friend. Not any more. He doesn't have a best friend.

Sarah Ann is in her black stage. She's wearing black jeans, sneakers, shirt and danglies. Her lips are black and so are the deep shadows above and below her eyes.

She holds up a finger and turns from her machines.

"Mom's at a meeting and Mike's got a job, so I'm in charge."

Bennie knows better than to say anything.

"Felice and Tania are coming over and I don't want you hanging around downstairs," his sister says. "I don't want you in my hair."

Her hair is also black, unnaturally so, dyed within an inch of its life. She wears sparklies in it.

"So get your sandwich or whatever and bring it up and stay in here."

She flounces off her bed, leaving it littered with McCrap, school books, socks (black) and cosmetics.

Great. Stay put, but stay out of the way. It'll be a fun night. Just you wait.

On campus Ray is invisible. He blends into the background like plants or stacks of books. He limps around the small school—cleaning, picking up, fixing up, standing aside during recess or lunch periods.

Most of the kids and teachers don't see him at all, although they pass him in the hall several times each day.

Nobody says hello. Nobody knows his name. Ray doesn't care. He's grateful for the work, for the place to stay, for the peace if not the quiet.

He wouldn't know quite what to do with complete quiet. He didn't do well with the antiseptic silence in the hospitals. But he also has trouble with the pressure and tension of city life. The bustle of school life is perfect.

Something about children's voices, their screams, their laughter—it's soothing to Ray.

It's a rainy night. You can hear it on the tin roof of the trailer, a constant tempo against the bolder beats of the heavy metal on the old-fashioned stereo. Ray likes his music really cranked.

He's toiling at his tiny fold-up table, bent over his work. The place is very crowded, mostly with Giants memorabilia. There are Giants cards, Giants calendars, Giants cups and Giants caps. All the higher shelves display bobbleheads of different Giants players, including some who haven't played in more than a decade.

Ray is tinkering, thinkering. He pauses from time to time and just looks down at the table. It holds the old computer he got when the school re-tooled, the scanner he picked up at a garage sale, scissors and paste. Is that an old Monopoly board?

It's painstaking work, whatever it is he's doing. He's downloading images, sizing them, printing them. Small scraps of paper litter the floor and paste is spilled on the table.

He wasn't always like this, so laid back. Before the Gulf War, he was the guy in his company who knew how to get things done. He was a sportsman who loved a good game and a good time.

Then came the war. Then came the limp. Then a life of not getting things done. There were stints as a baker, as a delivery driver, as a park ranger. No more guns. No more parties. Too lame. Too tame for such things now.

Then there was Bayshore Intermediate, a safe place, a soft landing. A good school, good for Ray. Good for Bayshore too. He's dependable and available 24-7 because he lives on site.

And then Bennie.

What if you were easy to not notice?

Ray notices. He sees Bennie trying not to be seen, staying in the middle of the pack or toward the back. Ray knows about invisible. He can see the invisible people.

He can see Bennie.

He has a clear image of the boy in his mind as he continues his toils amid the thunderous drums and the tinny patter. The tiny trailer rides the rainy night.

A steady drizzle now, nothing dramatic, just universal dampness. But Bennie's having a first-rate day anyway, thanks to Ms. Robertson. She came up to him after first period PE with a baseball glove.

He doesn't take it off his hand until school's over. He holds it under his desk during class, smiling to himself through the lessons, ducking his head and sneaking smells. He loves the leathery odor, the outdoorsy tang, the delicious sweet oil. At lunch, he eats one-handed.

After school he tucks it under his jacket so it won't get wet. He ducks across the parking lot and into the public library. He brushes his Giants cap against his leg to get the water off it. The librarian looks up and smiles at him. He comes almost every day lately.

Holding the glove between his legs, Bennie gets on the internet. He searches baseball topics—how to care for gloves, how to play infield, Barry Bonds on hitting.

Back at the apartment, Mike wants to know where Bennie got the glove. He grabs it and waves it just out of Bennie's reach.

"Where does a kid like you get something like this?" he taunts. "Who'd you steal this from?"

"Give it to me? Give to me! It's a loan. I'm responsible for it."

"A loan? From who? From your local sporting goods store?"

"From the PE teacher. She told me I could use it."

"I'll bet," Mike says, inspecting the glove. "Pretty good merchandise. I might want to use it myself, take it to a Giants game." Mike gives Bennie an evil glare.

"Let me have it!"

"Listen, kid," he throws the glove at the boy's feet. "Don't you talk to me that way. Not ever! You understand me?" He pokes his finger two inches from Bennie's face.

Bennie nods, miserable. He feels like the weather.

He stands at the back window, looking out at the antenna farm in soft focus. He punches the glove. His fist is about the size of the baseball now. It fits the pocket perfectly.

Rain blurs the tall towers in the PG&E yard, illuminated by searchlights on the square brick substation. The tops disappear in the darkness.

He's punches the glove, hitting it hard, hitting it again. He wishes it were Mike.

He's staring into the rain. The struts on the towers glisten faintly in the wet night. The day had started so well.

He's hating Mike, wishing he'd never met the man.

He's punching the glove. Hard.

It's a board game. Ray shows up at the library on a rainy Saturday because he knows that's where the boy will be and asks him to play.

"No thanks." Bennie mumbles, embarrassed to be approached by an adult.

"It's about baseball," Ray says.

"Not interested." Although Bennie is, a little.

"Too bad, you'd probably be good at it," Ray says, opening the board. It looks like a baseball diamond. "It teaches about the game. "

"How?"

"Teaches you how to think."

"I dunno …"

"C'mon. You'd do me a favor," Ray says. "You don't have anything else to do today, do you? It took me forever to put this thing together."

"Maybe for a few minutes."

"I love a good game." Ray is rubbing his hands together.

He sets up in one of the study rooms. He puts piles of cards on both sides of the board and in the middle. He's created cards for each member of each major league team. That was most of the work.

Ray explains that each player assembles a new major league team and then manages it. He hands Bennie a pair of dice and details the rules.

"You can really learn a lot about strategy and tactics," he says. "I call it … Big League Ball."

Bennie starts sifting through the stack of player cards.

"Let's try it," he says.

The first game takes almost two hours. Ray's Rangers pull out a 9-8 victory over Bennie's Bombers. In the last three innings, Bennie really gets into the game. He's disappointed to lose.

"You didn't want me to let you win?" Ray asks, all innocence.

In the second game, there's a lot of tabletalk, some handslaps and some headslaps too. The man gets to be like a boy for a few minutes, to laugh and lose himself in the competition. The boy gets to feel like a man and to win, a rare thing for him.

Bennie spends many hours mastering the game. He plays Ray whenever he can, usually two or three times each week. They set up in one of the classrooms after school.

He also plays by himself in his room, careful to keep the cards and board out of sight when Mike's around. Sarah Ann isn't interested, but she won't disturb the board, even when Bennie leaves a game in progress.

Sometimes he gets sick of Big League Ball too. Good as it is, it's not the real thing. It's not the same as baseball.

Sometimes he's drawn outdoors, regardless of the weather, to try to find someplace, anyplace, where he can get in a little exercise. The yard next to the library is full of pools of standing water, so he goes back to the pocket park.

The net is down on the tennis court. He can play against that practice wall without obstruction. He finds a good spot, winds up and throws the tennis ball as hard as he can.

Splat. It hits the wall, bounces onto the sodden concrete and skids into a standing pool.

Bennie picks it up and squeezes the ball. A few drops come out.

He throws again and tries to field the bounce. Right through a puddle. *Squish.* His shoes make a wet sound with each step.

The ball gets heavier. The rebounds get shorter until the ball sort of slides down the wall and doesn't bounce at all.

Bennie is truly sick of the rain.

A clear day. A warm afternoon. Finally.

As school lets out, kids are taking off their jackets and taking their time clearing the yard. Bennie is impatient. He stands against the back fence, tossing a baseball into his glove.

A real ball, not a tennis ball. Ray gave it to him, saying: "You can't use a tennis ball with a glove like that."

None of the other students takes any notice of Bennie. But Ray does. He's cleaning up the trash in the yard. He nods a greeting.

Bennie holds up the ball, but Ray shakes his head and holds up his broom.

"Must be spring," Vera says, peering out her window.

As Bennie takes his position opposite the library wall, he notices that the pole holding the basketball backboard has been removed. There's a circle of darker concrete where it used to be. That will make it a little easier for him.

Bennie winds up and throws the ball with as much authority as he can muster.

Donk.

It comes back fairly slowly, not nearly as quickly as the tennis ball. The baseball is heavier, the wall not a wonderful bouncing surface.

The boy sets himself and throws again, concentrating.

Bam.

No doubt that the baseball sounds different than the tennis ball too. Inside the library, the principal tries to calm the librarian.

Bam.

"This is not acceptable," the librarian says, agitated, wiping perspiration from her upper lip.

Thump.

"I know it's hard for you." Norm tries to look sympathetic.

Thump.

"What about my after school reading group?"

"Couldn't you meet inside in one of the classrooms, just for a little while?"

BAM!

"Last year ... I don't know ... half as loud."

BAM!

4

SIXTH GRADE, his second year at the wall, his after school ritual.

Bennie sets up outside the library and starts throwing, catching the rebounds. It's his warm-up exercise. He's at ease now. All the school staff know him and expect him to be there.

Ray grabs a ball that gets past the boy and underhands it to him.

"Never make the Giants like that," he jokes as he continues his clean-up of the yard.

Bennie is still working on his pitching. When he feels loose, he takes his place on the small concrete circle where the backboard pole used to be. He's trying to hit a smudge about three feet up on the wall.

He goes into his windup again and throws and notices out of the corner of his eye …

Ken Sato, leaning on the fence, watching.

"Hey."

"Hey."

Ken just stands there. Normally he's halfway up the hill by this time, climbing the steep street around the corner from Bayshore Intermediate.

"You … need something?" Bennie asks.

Ken shakes his head.

Although the two boys are in the same grade, they don't know each other very well. They have different teachers. Ken hangs with his own crowd, mostly Asian and white kids who live in the expensive split-level homes at the top of the hill.

Bennie belongs to the bottom-of-the-hill culture, the people who live in the apartments or the rundown streets on either side of Geneva. No grocery stores. Only fast food and booze.

Everyone has to wear the same uniform, so social boundaries aren't very visible during the school day. But they're there, two distinct worlds with a small school shared between them. You see it in the lunchroom or on the playground, where students form their own groups based on where they live.

And you see it on the neighborhood streets when the kids walk home. The Taco Man parks his shiny aluminum cart just off school grounds, where he can push his sugary drinks and high-fat snacks to the hungry kids as they leave campus. The ones who can afford it are the ones who walk uphill, but they usually don't stop at the roach coach, as they call it.

There are no sports teams at Bayshore, where top-of-the-hill kids and bottom-of-the-hill kids might integrate in common cause. The school is too poor to provide buses for any interleague play. So it's a little strange, these two boys, standing there on the after school asphalt.

After tossing the ball into his mitt a few times, Bennie turns back to the wall. He throws and misses wide by about two feet.

The other boy sits on his bulging knapsack.

Bennie gets the ball and throws again. This time he misses high. It doesn't make it any easier to have Sato staring at him.

A third throw goes left.

"Your motion is wrong."

"Huh? What do you mean?" Bennie turns to Ken.

"Your motion is pulling you off your target."

"How so?" Bennie asks.

Ken trots over to the fence and retrieves the ball. He walks up to Bennie and gestures for him to step aside. A little surprised, Bennie moves.

Ken throws and hits the smudge in the exact center.

"That's the right motion," he says.

He fields the bounce barehanded and throws again. The ball goes left.

"That's the wrong motion."

Ken trots to the ball and brings it back. He flips it to Bennie.

"How do you know that?" Bennie asks.

"Been watching you." Ken points up the hill toward a house with a terraced back lawn. "You sure like baseball."

"Yeah ...so? "

"I like baseball too," he grins. "A lot."

"But how do you know about the motion?"

"Oh, well, I'm a pitcher."

"A pitcher? Where?"

"I play in the Little League in San Mateo. Wednesdays and Saturdays."

Bennie hasn't been in a league for years, not since he was eight years old and his mom was married. No way to get to the games. No money for uniforms and equipment from his two-job, single-parent mom. He tosses the ball in the air a couple times, before he flips it back to Ken.

"Show me?"

The boys play the wall together the next day and the two days after that.

Ken explains his pitching motion to Bennie. He learned from his Dad, who played in college in Japan. It's all about balance and timing, how to create and to control the force behind each throw.

Ken is a natural athlete. His windup is compact and powerful, his throws accurate, his fielding effortless. His body always seems to know what to do.

Bennie has trouble getting his arms and legs to do exactly the same thing twice in a row.

They take turns throwing and retrieving. They make a game of it. They draw a chalk outline of the strike zone around the smudge on the wall. The one who isn't throwing is the umpire, calling balls and strikes.

"Strike three. He's outa there," Ken declares, moving to his right to get the bounce.

They agree not to argue the umpire's decisions. They are scrupulously fair with each other.

"Top of the fifth," Ken announces, taking his place at the "mound." The rubber is a scrap of cardboard in the middle of the concrete circle.

They keep at it until Ken has to go home and then resume as soon as they can the next afternoon. Ken is way ahead, but Bennie eventually wins a few games. He works hard, copying Ken's throwing motion, and he improves.

On the fourth day, about a half-hour in, the librarian appears and she's got the principal with her.

"Too loud," she says, wiping perspiration from her lip. "Too much with two of you. Bam! Bam! Bam! Too much!"

Norm likes to avoid problems. He has a solution.

"Why can't you throw to each other now?" he suggests.

Bennie looks down, unable to meet the principal's gentle gaze. He stamps both sneakered feet in his nervousness.

"It's only been this week," he manages.

"It's always been OK to play against the library," Ken adds.

Norm holds up his hand when the librarian wants to respond. He makes the boys wait for one long sigh.

"There are two of you now," he says. "Don't use the wall. OK? Clear?"

And the boys have to agree. They share a grin.

Ray watches from the upper yard. A rueful smile flickers across his features. Bennie has found a friend. Ray has found a candy wrapper. He bends to pick it up.

The boys try playing catch with each other, as the principal suggested, but it isn't easy. There isn't enough room in the lower yard by the library (besides, Norm frowns whenever he sees them). In the upper yard, the ball skips into thick, sharp bushes if they muff a catch.

They try the street, but traffic constantly interrupts their games. Misses roll forever or until they wind up underneath a car, sometimes moving. Other kids stop by to watch or talk or just generally distract them. They're not exactly welcoming to Ken.

"Why don't you stay in your own neighborhood, Sato?" Franklin is a stocky seventh grader who lives in the same apartments as Bennie.

So it's up the hill, the first time for Bennie. There was never any reason before. He never considered it part of his neighborhood.

The climb is an adventure in itself. It's quite an incline, steep as a playground slide, too steep to stop quickly going up or down, walking or driving.

Ken's two neighbors do their best to put Bennie in his place.

"Hey, Sato, is this your caddy?" asks Tim Shu, who's in Bennie's class.

"You don't have a caddy for baseball," says Mike Chan, a fifth-grader.

Bennie is carrying his own glove and ball. He's the shortest of the group, the only one without jet black hair.

"Give 'im your backpack, Kenny," Shu says. "Why should you lug it up the hill? In fact, why should I?"

He stops and tosses his backpack at Bennie's feet.

"Go eat a Big Mac, Shu," Ken says casually. Tim is a little chunky and he's huffing from the exertion.

Bennie steps easily over Tim's backpack. He tries to banter with Shu.

"If you just sit down, you could roll all the way to Mickey D's," he giggles at his own joke.

Tim is offended. It's one thing for Ken to jab at his weight, but another thing entirely for this flatlander to do it.

"Listen, shithead, how'd you like to roll right back where you belong?"

"I just ...," Bennie begins.

Ken cuts it off with a look and a headshake. He waits for Bennie to catch up to him.

"Don't pay any attention to them," he says.

Bennie takes in the view near the top. He can see over the treetops and beyond the antenna farm to San Francisco Bay in the distance. It's a different world from the flats. There's a sense of space. The houses are twice the size of the ones down below. They have yards and shiny paint. There are no apartments up here.

Bennie follows Ken to an empty lot sandwiched between two houses built right to the edge of their property lines.

"What do you think?" Ken asks.

"Makes me miss the schoolyard."

They laugh. Empty is a misleading term for the lot. Bushes occur randomly across the expanse. Scrap papers and other trash are scattered all over the place. There's more junk hidden under the long grass.

For the next week, the boys spend every afternoon at work. They clear out a dozen bags of trash, some tin cans and several stickery shrubs. They stuff them in garbage bags they haul to Ken's house. They yank or scythe most of the tall yellow grasses and trample the rest. It's dirty, painstaking labor that leaves them with blisters on their hands and scratched arms.

It also leaves them with a field. They still have to deal with random gopher holes and uneven terrain, but they have a place they can play. It feels like a stadium to them.

They decide to launch the World Catch Championships. One person throws and the other catches. The thrower tries to put the ball as far as he can from the fielder, but it still has to be catchable. They keep score—an out for a catch, three outs an inning. Every missed catch is counted as a single. The winner is the one who scores the most runs.

They begin about 10 feet from each other and they gradually get farther and farther back. As the game progresses, the thrower backs down the street, while the fielder stays on the lot.

"A screamer to right field," Ken calls the play. "Bruno is over. He's under it. He's got ...wait, he dropped it. The ball goes behind him. The runner pulls into second."

Bennie tosses the ball back and Ken heaves a high one.

Bennie takes off to his left and makes a spectacular rolling catch.

"Haaahhhh!" Ken exhales the crowd noise. "The fans go wild! A superhuman effort."

Bennie's turn to throw. He takes over the announcer's role too.

"Top of the fifth now. Bruno at the plate. He swings at the first pitch."

He heaves a line drive far to Ken's right. Ken starts slowly and reaches for the ball, only to have it tip off his glove.

"It's a hit!" Bennie shouts.

On the next throw, Ken trips in a hole in the field and goes sprawling.

"All right! A run for the good guys," Bennie cheers.

The way they play is the basis of their relationship. They push each other. They take it seriously. After all, it's baseball. They both agree they're soon-to-be best on the planet, so their play is important. At least to them.

Ken gets up, making a "T" with both hands to call time out. He invites Bennie back to his place for a snack.

Bennie has never been inside a house as large as Sato's split-level. There are four bedrooms, a family room and a garage. Ken's mom and dad share an office in the guest bedroom, where Mr. Sato is working behind a closed door.

"Nice to meet you, Bennie," Mrs. Sato says, looking up from her reading and offering her hand. She's sitting at the table in the large, sunny kitchen. "I always like to meet Ken's friends."

Bennie mumbles something and misses the handshake, too shy to look directly at the woman. Ken grins and shrugs at his mom.

Ken's kid sister, Angie, has a room crammed with stuffed animals. There must be 300 of them.

"She's at a friend's place." Ken explains.

The walls in Ken's room are covered with posters of the Giants.

"We went twice last week," he says.

Bennie hasn't been to a game in years.

"Not since I was little," he shakes his head. "Can't afford it."

On to Andy, Ken's terrier, frantic but friendly. Andy's idea of heaven is someone scratching his ears.

And on to ping pong, another first for Bennie. Ken explains the rules and plays an easy game to demonstrate the scoring.

Ken is expert. He plays the big table hard and fast. He moves around the family room with authority, slamming the ball with full-arm swings. He demolishes Bennie.

Bennie tries backing up, only to have Ken drop the ball barely over the net. Up and back, side to side, up and back. Bennie's sweating and Ken isn't even breathing hard.

"You want me to go easy?" Ken the Merciless.

"No, thanks. Gimme whatcha got."

Bennie takes his beating. He thoroughly enjoys it.

School's out for the summer and Bennie adopts a play-and-stay strategy.

Play baseball. As much as he can. As many ways as he can.

Stay away from the apartment. Stay away from Mike. Stay out of sight.

If he attracts attention at home, he gets chores. Household stuff that Sarah Ann has ducked or that Ma didn't get to because she's so busy or that Mike dumped because he's so lazy. Drop the dry cleaning. Get a few groceries from the mini-mart (and lug them home). Deal with the garbage. Dishes.

And he gets questions he didn't get when school was in session. Where are you going? What're you doing? What? What? What?

Who needs that?

So Bennie is up and out early, quick and quiet. It's cold and foggy most summer mornings in Daly City. He dresses in layers.

Most weekdays he goes by the daycare center at his old elementary school, where he helps out with the little kids on the playground before indoor activities start. There's an aide there, Ms. Spaulding, who lives in the same apartments. She gives Bennie a breakfast tray if there's any left. There almost always is.

He tells Ma he's got a job. He doesn't say it pays in eats or that it's over by 8:30. He's too young to get a work permit anyway.

Then he drifts toward Geneva, the main drag, where the buses glide back and forth on overhead lines. A lot of local people go to work in SF. A few students are boarding buses to go to summer school across town. There aren't any classes at Bayshore this summer.

Bennie cruises through MacDonald's, the premier eatery in the district. He can usually find a sports section, so he can read about yesterday's games. And a bathroom if he needs it.

By this time, it's warming up. Bennie goes back to Bayshore and gets loose by throwing against the library wall. He can do it because nobody's around, except Ray, and he doesn't mind. He waves at Bennie in a friendly way, but he's always got work to do, even during the summer break.

Ken sleeps in. He stays up late when he doesn't have to go to school. He doodles around online on the social sites or he watches the tube. Or he plays video games with his neighbors, Tim or sometimes Eddie Wang, a seventh-grader.

The guys go to Giants games together. At least once each week during the summer, Ken goes to the movies with them. Or they bus to the mall and just wander around.

Bennie never comes on these expeditions. He won't let Ken pay his way. Ken doesn't push it. He figures it's a pride thing.

Ken gets going slowly. He likes a big breakfast and then he takes a shower. It's at least 10 o'clock before he ambles out to the vacant lot. Sometimes later.

Bennie is already there. Always.

When Ken isn't around, Bennie tries to take advantage of the time. He works hard at making his pitching better. After thousands of throws against the schoolyard wall, he begins to find some force, unwinding his skinny 12-year-old frame, but his control still leaves a lot to be desired.

On days when Ken is with his other friends, Bennie finds ways to improve his defense. He goes to the practice wall at the pocket park and he discovers something about himself he didn't expect. He's still afraid of the ball. Not like when he was younger, but it's still there. He recognizes an occasional flinch, a flicker of terror that the ball will hurt him.

He faces down his fear by playing three feet away from the wall. He's forced to make instant reactions. There isn't time to be afraid. He gets a face full of bruises. He learns that the dings to his forehead or chin aren't that bad, although bloody noses aren't much fun. Overall, it's minor.

Ken notices the bumps and bangs, but he doesn't say anything about them. He admires Bennie's unusual intensity, his dedication to baseball. How does he know what he wants so young? Ken doesn't quite understand.

Ken has a nice home, a two-parent family and plenty of money. He's good-looking, popular and smart. All that and he's gifted with athletic ability.

To Bennie, it looks like Ken has all the answers. But he doesn't. He has no direction. Ken has so many questions ....

Who do I want to be?

Who cares which superhero is best?

Why is it fun to kill (digital) aliens?

What's so wonderful about wearing out your thumbs tapping tiny text messages? Why not just talk to people?

And what have I gotten myself into with this Bruno kid?

Bennie never says anything, but he's always waiting at the lot.

I'll never get rid of him, Ken thinks. Do I want to?

Bennie never pressures, but Ken feels pressure. Bennie is always somewhere practicing. The man is a maniac at getting his game.

Am I going to let him get to be a better ballplayer than me?

Baseball or free time?

Bennie or the other guys? No one likes him. He's got no other friends. He's a social zero. He can't talk about anything but baseball. You almost have to feel sorry for him.

Yet Ken finds himself looking forward to finding him at the empty lot.

"Hey, Bennie, what do you say?"

There's nowhere at the apartment where Bennie is completely comfortable.

He sleeps in the dining area, which is actually the narrow end of the living room. He puts up a shower curtain for privacy. He stashes his clothes in cardboard boxes pushed against the wall. He keeps his schoolwork on the dinette table, careful to leave one half free in case anyone wants to use it for eating. People usually eat in front of the TV.

He moved because Sarah Ann decided she needed the whole bedroom to herself. The real reason she kicked Bennie out was so she could lock the door.

"Can't do that if you're in here."

Bennie argued, pled that he didn't mind, promised he'd keep the door locked all the time. Sarah Ann wouldn't hear of it.

Three years older, some days Sarah Ann looks 10 years older. She looks like she could be Bennie's young mother until you look closely and see under all the cosmetics she's wearing.

She pretends to be so tough, but really she's a scared little girl. The week before, Mike came after her when Bennie was in the room. He was drunk and he just jumped on top of her. She was busy texting someone and didn't see him coming. He knocked her phone onto the floor and it skidded under Bennie's bed.

Mike turned to Bennie and said: "Git! Now!"

Sarah Ann was kicking and screaming and punching. She told her brother not to go.

"Get 'im off me! Get 'im off me! Call the cops!"

Bennie reached under his bed for the phone. Mike backed off Sarah Ann.

"Geez, I was only jokin'," he said and then he shook his finger at Bennie. "I'm warnin' you. Don't you ever."

He didn't have to finish that sentence. He left and slammed the door—hard—to show what a big man he was.

Sarah Ann was sobbing. She grabbed Bennie by the shoulders.

"Don't you say anything about this, not to Mom, not to any-body," she insisted, still crying. "Promise? You promise?"

Bennie's big sister used to be his best friend. He looked up to her. She was his protector. She provided a place where he could shelter when storms broke across the apartment. Now the roles are reversing. He tries to keep his sister safe. He gives up his own space.

Downstairs is noisy for Bennie. Mike watches TV with the volume turned up until 1 a.m. every night.

And it's bad right now between him and Ma. They shout at each other or they won't speak to each other at all. Then they order Bennie to tell something to the other one. He doesn't like getting caught in the middle of these silent arguments. Loud silence for him.

Bennie hates their fights. His stomach knots at the thought that Mike might hurt his mother. He hates Mike.

When it's not too foggy, Bennie sometimes sleeps on the tiny porch off the back of the apartment, overlooking the antenna farm. It's damp out there, but he can close the glass doors and cut off some of the sound.

Ma and Sarah Ann sleep behind separate closed doors. Mike is usually snoring on the living room couch when Bennie wakes up.

He tiptoes past him.

The two boys become inseparable. They play baseball, watch it, talk it, practice it, listen to it, and play it some more. It's the topic underneath everything they discuss. When they eat, they are consumed by baseball. When they sleep, they dream of baseball. Baseball is what they do. It's all they do.

They play pitch, the catcher making the ball or strike call. Ken always wins. He's starting to find his curve.

They play catch. They trade the World Championship back and forth many times. Bennie proves himself a little better in the field.

They discover how different it is to play a batted ball. They toss the ball up with one hand and hit flies and grounders to each other.

When they're finished for the day, they go back to Ken's room and watch a game on TV, usually the Giants. They play Big League Ball, Ray's game, and they stage a summer-long festival of old baseball movies.

If they're not together, Bennie listens to the Giants game. Really listens. He huddles on that tiny porch, overlooking the antenna farm, wrapped in blankets to keep warm. He listens to every pitch.

One Sunday, they hop a Samtrans bus to Caltrain and take the train to China Basin. They join the thousands streaming toward the Giants game.

The redbrick ballpark is nestled against San Francisco Bay. The statue of Willie Mays, finishing his remarkable home run swing, dominates the front plaza. Around back, the ferry is just arriving from Sausalito, passengers pouring down the wobbly gangway. Ken leads Bennie to the right-field wall, where there are archways opening onto the entire field. You can watch for free.

"What do you think?"

"Neat. I didn't know you could do this."

Between innings, the boys put their feet on the guardrails and watch the kayaks and small boats in McCovey Cove. They cross the short bridge to inspect the Willie McCovey statue on the other side. They wander over by the marina, but they can't get past the locked gates.

After the game, the boys stop at Yerba Buena and spend a half-hour watching a bluegrass band performing on the stage at the park. Some people are dancing in the grass. Others are sleeping in the warm afternoon. The boys caper across San Francisco, heading back downtown to catch the train back home.

They've only traveled five miles from Bayshore, but it's all new for Bennie.

On the other hand, his reception when he arrives back at the apartment is getting old.

"Where've you been all day?" Mike confronts him as he walks in the door. "What've you been doin'?"

"Dunno. Nothing. Hang."

There goes that good mood.

"With that hoity-toity Japanese kid?"

"No … not always … sometimes."

"Keep away from those people. They look down their noses at folks like us."

"They're not like that."

"It's for your own good, Bennie," Ma chimes in.

Bennie nods and studies the floor. He doesn't want to look at them. When they turn away, he's gone.

Bennie unlocks the garage door and lets himself in. Andy runs up and jumps on his leg.

Bennie pets the little dog for a couple minutes. He goes to the Sato's cupboard and gets food for the animal. After Andy eats, Bennie lets him into the fenced backyard, so he can do his business. Bennie's getting five dollars a day to take care of the dog while the Satos are visiting family back east.

While he's waiting, Bennie goes into the family room. He pulls one end of the ping pong table up into a vertical position and leaves the other side down. As he stands at the end of the table, he's facing a big green wall with white stripes on it.

He serves the ball. It bounces back very quickly. It's like having someone standing at the net, like standing close to the wall at the pocket park. Bennie earns small red circles on his arms and forehead from missed returns.

But he gets a feel for the timing in a few minutes. He experiments with how to hold the paddle and strike the ball. He is, as you might expect, intent.

Bennie keeps at it. He gets so he can return his own serves. By accident, he discovers how to spin the ball by making a sideways motion with the paddle. He sees how differently a spun ball bounces. Interesting possibilities, he thinks.

Andy wants to be let in. How long has he been barking?

Bennie is invited to watch a couple of Ken's Pony League games. He rides down the Peninsula with the entire Sato family.

Sarah Ann agrees to cover for him. She goes out with her friends most evenings. She'll tell Ma that Bennie came with them to the movies. They'll hook up afterward at McDee's so they can go home together. The arrangement costs Bennie a few extra chores.

The Pony League is pretty fancy. All the teams are complete, nine boys on the field at one time, wearing expensive uniforms supplied by local business sponsors. The field is in great shape. It's a far cry from the pockmarked lot, where Bennie and Ken usually do battle.

Ken is better than most of the players. He can do what he tries to do. His fastball overpowers most of the other boys. His curve, honed with Bennie, completely puzzles his opponents. He doesn't lose his head when a ball is hit toward him. There are only one or two boys like him in the league.

After the games, Mr. Sato treats both boys to the batting machines. It's one gift that Bennie can't bear to refuse.

"You seem to see the ball pretty well," Mr. Sato tells him as he takes a few swings against the pitching machine. "But you're not hitting it squarely. Your swing is off."

Bennie concentrates on the tips Mr. Sato gives him. Within a half hour, he feels his swing start to improve.

Comes the evening that Ken's team needs a player. They had lost too many boys to family vacations and were faced with a forfeit if they couldn't field a full team. Bennie is the answer. The elated answer.

They give him an extra uniform. It's too big and Ken's mom pins it up for Bennie. He can feel the tiny metal posts against his ankles, wrists and waist. The shirt slides around on his shoulders. Bennie thinks it's grand.

This is his first real game, his first time in uniform since he was a little kid. His first time at bat against anyone except Ken or a pitching machine. His first time to have a field full of people trying to catch what he hits.

He's so excited he can hardly stand still in the batter's box. His first time up, he makes it to second on a slow grounder to third. It should be an out, but it's a long throw across the diamond and the ball skips past the first baseman.

Standing at second, Bennie studies the opposing pitcher, a guy named Lacey. He realizes the boy only has one pitch. He has all he can do to get the ball over the plate. Bennie can pitch better than he can.

Bennie murders him the next time up, slamming a double into left field. He doesn't see another ball he can reach. Lacey walks him the next three times at bat.

The game is a huge rush for Bennie. He's more in love with baseball than ever. But it's harder to have those stay-at-home evenings, listening to the Giants on the tiny porch, trying not to think about Ken at his Pony League game.

And it's harder to go back to two-man baseball. For the first time, Bennie understands why Ken gets bored sometimes when just the two of them are playing.

The boys decide to hunt for a game. They ride the buses all over the Upper Mission and Daly City, even down into Pacifica. They check schools and parks, using a map they get on the web. All they can find are league contests on weekday evenings and Saturdays. Nothing during weekdays. No pick-up games, no neighborhood kids getting together on the spur on the moment. Only for basketball.

"My dad says kids play all over the place in Japan," Ken says.

"Ray says it was like that here when he was growing up," says Bennie.

Then they happen onto Crocker Park. It's just a stone's throw from Bayshore, three minutes on the bus, but it's tucked back off Geneva and hard to see. It's much larger than the map indicates. There are several basketball courts and a community center. And two fields for baseball, complete with backstops and chalked baselines.

A dozen kids are engaged in a game. They're all Latinos and they all know each other. They heckle and hassle each other. They argue and tease. They're their own fans. There are no uniforms except torn jeans and worn equipment. A couple outfielders have no gloves, so the opposing fielders let them use theirs.

The play is enthusiastic. It's at a higher level than Ken's Pony League teams.

Bennie and Ken hold back, shy about intruding. They watch from 50 yards away and gradually get closer. By the end of the first day, they're near the outfield foul lines. The ballplayers see them, standing there with their gloves, but they don't pay any attention. They go on with their game.

The players are mixed ages. There are a few older kids. They take the key positions like pitcher and catcher. When a younger kid comes up to bat, the pitcher throws easy ones to him, sometimes underhanded.

Bennie and Ken go home without speaking to anyone, but they come back at about the same time the next day. By the end of the second day, they're watching from a few feet into foul territory. They're close enough so they laugh along with some of the players. Ken cheers some good plays, but Bennie is still too shy to talk.

On the fourth day, the neighborhood kids ask Bennie and Ken to join the game.

But it doesn't really work out for them, although the Crocker boys are too polite to say so, at least directly. They're both nervous and they don't play as well as they can. They don't quite fit in.

They don't know their teammates' names. They don't get a lot of the Spanish slang, so they miss some of the jokes.

Maybe that's on purpose.

Bennie makes four outs at bat and three errors in the field. Ken gets on base twice, but he gets caught in a rundown once.

They don't go back to Crocker that summer.

They try to work on their hitting, but it's frustrating with only two players. If one pitches and the other bats, there's no one left to catch. If the batter swings and misses, he has to chase the ball. If the batter hits the ball, the pitcher has to chase it.

No fun.

"This sucks," Ken says after lunch. "Let's go down to your place for a change."

"Can't. Mike might be there."

"We'll go to your room. We'll stay out of his way."

"No room, Kenny."

"You mean, you still share with your sister?"

"Sleepin' in the corner of the living room."

"Oh …"

"Mike drinks in the afternoons," Bennie adds.

He never had a close friend before—someone he could spend time with, someone he could tell personal stuff. They don't need to say much.

"Oh, yeah …"

Sometimes they talk without even talking. When an everyday topic comes up—say the way the Giants are playing—Ken can turn and just look at Bennie. They know what each other thinks about everything.

Without a word, they decide to go back to the lot, back to the World Catch Championships, now at Inning 540.

They play for hours. Bennie is bruised. His shirt is smeared with dirt. Ken's normally neat hair is everywhere. His knees are grass-stained. Both boys move like they're tired.

It's 5-5, bottom of the 14th (554th) inning and it's getting late. Twilight's coming a little earlier now.

Ken is "up." He throws a blooper, purposely short, toward right field. Bennie breaks a beat too late. He bends so low his glove is scooping the grass, but the ball short-hops and hits him in the knee.

"Ouch!" he says. "That's a runner on second."

Ken throws again, a high one straight up. Bennie looks skyward, but can't find the ball. He notices a few stars. He starts to back up uncertainly.

"I … I can't see it."

The ball plops 10 feet in front of him.

"Called on account of darkness," Ken hollers, laughing and tossing his glove in the air.

The game ends. So too their summer. Seventh grade begins.

5

COACH WALKS ACROSS the room, carrying paper and tape. He stops at the rook's open locker. Bruno is still in the shower.

Coach slams the door, drawing everyone's attention. Using wide, bright blue tape—lots of it—he fixes a single sheet to the outside of the locker. The display is hard to miss.

He glares at Bruno, just toweling off, but doesn't say anything. He grabs his tape and stomps out, not looking at anybody, leaving a wake like bad weather.

"Hoooeee," says Devon, shaking his fingers and blowing on them. "He's hot! You got some trouble, boy."

"I'm not trying to make trouble," Bennie says.

Devon leans in. "It's the signs. He's posted the signs. Ha!" He wags his finger. "Kissin' off the coach like that. That's gonna have to stop."

"Yeah," Pedro says, "Skip's lettin' you swat the ball the way you want. What's the problem with the signs?"

"It doesn't work for me," Bennie says. "I just can't do what he tells me."

"It's part of the game," Pedro says. "It's expected."

"It's different with my twisty hits. I can't tell what I can do until I see the pitch. So how can he tell me what to do?"

"What do you mean?" Pedro asks.

"When I put a spin on the ball, where it goes depends on which way the pitch is spinning in the first place. Say the pitch is spinning right or clockwise, then it's almost impossible to bunt it to the right side. It'll go out of bounds."

"You can actually see which way the pitch is spinning?" Devon asks, wide-eyed.

"Sure. Can't you?"

Johnnie laughs. He can see the pitch spin now too. Bennie showed him some eye exercises and his batting average has gone up 20 points because of it. He and Bennie are now hitting number one and number two.

He steps in to defend his friend. "We all know why he gets away with it. Skip won't shut down the team engine."

Some loud exhales, some head shakes.

It becomes a clubhouse discussion. What about those hand signals? Who decides what a batter does?

It goes on for days when Skip and Coach aren't around. It's informal. It's available to anyone who's interested.

"We win or lose together," says Frankie. "That's more important than individual stats."

"Nobody is disputing that," Johnnie says. "We'd all do that. We'd give up an out to move a runner. It's a decision the individual makes for his team."

It's not that people sit in a big circle and raise their hands and take turns. It happens as the guys take their showers, get dressed or oil their gloves.

"That's a decision Skip and Coach make for the team," says Carlos, as he dries off his dark hair. "Then they send us the signals."

"Baseball is a complicated game," says T.J., the catcher and team captain. "Leave those decisions to them. It's their job."

Back and forth, the debate continues. It deepens. It divides. It unites. It spreads into every corner of the locker room. Pretty soon, the whole team is involved.

"Why do they get to decide?" Johnnie asks. "We're the ones at the plate."

"They've got a lot more experience than we do," Frankie says. "They got strategies."

"It's their team," says Winston.

"It's our team." Johnnie says.

"That's right," Juan agrees. "We're the team. Why should they tell us what to do?"

"Instead of us telling us what to do," Johnnie adds.

"That's assuming that we know better," Frankie says, "that we know enough to make the call."

"You're taking away one of the manager's most important tools," T.J. says, adjusting his hat, checking it out in the mirror.

"Why should we let them complicate the actual situation?" Bennie wonders.

"The actual situation?" Pedro asks.

"Throw the ball. Hit the ball." He's tying his shoes.

"Yeah, but you're putting your individual judgment against the team judgment, the skipper's judgment," Winston says.

"Most guys hate it when the skipper tells him what to do," Johnnie says.

"I hate it," Devon admits.

"I hate it," Pedro says.

"I like it," Juan says. "I don't have to think about what to do."

"I like to do my own thinking," Bennie says.

"If the kid can do it, I can too," Devon declares.

"Me too," says Juan.

Pedro is convinced. "I'll try it," he says.

Smitty follows the whole back-and-forth and doesn't say a word. The equipment manager is an oldtimer, quiet and constant, always there in the background. He scratches his stubble before he speaks. It's a surprise to hear his voice.

"Been waiting for years for something like this to happen."

A few of the guys laugh.

So the talk turns into action. The team is playing at home against the High Desert Mavericks. Pedro has a 3-0 count when Coach gives him the take sign.

Chin ear chin ear chin nose cap nose. Clap, Clap.

What Pedro takes is a vicious cut at a fat fastball. He hits it out of the park. As he trots around third, he won't look Coach in the eye.

The humidity is almost un … bear … able. It's a good thing the players don't wear fur. Rain threatens for the entire game.

Johnnie gets a take sign too.

Chin ear chin ear chin nose cap nose. Clap, Clap.

But he hits into a double play, instead of taking an almost certain walk.

Then Devon, then Juan—they step out on their own. They take a strike. They take a base. They take charge of their own at-bats.

Sometimes it works. Sometimes it doesn't.

"Give it time," Johnnie shouts from the shower after the game. "We gotta get used to it."

"One game doesn't prove anything," Pedro says.

"Remember, the pitcher wins two-thirds of the time," Devon says. "That's if you're good enough to bat .300 or higher."

It's an older/younger thing at first. The guys in their twenties (and Bennie) are into it. The players in their thirties hold back.

Next day, the boys are back at it. Johnnie steals a base when nobody is expecting it. Bennie ignores a bunt sign, of all things, and brings Johnnie home with a slash single past the drawn-in infield.

Juan grounds out and glances back at Coach as he runs back to the dugout. Somebody giggles on the bench.

"You people think it's funny?" Coach yells.

To say he's highly insulted doesn't begin to describe his reaction.

"What do you think you're doing?" he demands, sweat spraying from his head. "What do you think you're doing?"

He appeals to Skip: "How can you let this go on?"

"Micah, you just need to relax," Skip replies. "Let the line out. Just a little."

A full-scale player rebellion and Skip talks about fishing? Coach is stunned with anger, but the manager seems calm, almost amused.

"This is a learning experience," he informs his hitting instructor. Then adds, "For them."

Pedro runs through Coach's frantic stop sign at third and lumbers into an out at home. In despair, Coach turns away from the field of play.

"Chin up," Skip tells him, both men leaning on the dugout rail while the Bears are at bat. "You need to stay out there. Keep giving the signals. Keep giving them the right thing to do."

Coach does his best. He goes through all his motions, pumping his arms when the runners head toward home, flashing signs at runners, flashing signs at batters.

Signs the players don't bother to look at. Signs the players check and then forget.

It's something of a spectacle to the few who know what they're watching—Smitty and Burnside, the Bears announcer.

Skip is tugging his ears, pulling his chin, touching his arm, giving his commands from the dugout.

Coach is repeating the gestures. He's smiling. He's clapping. His stomach is churning. He wants to scream past his frozen smile.

He can't sleep. He can't get it out of his head. He dreams about the last game, the shame of being ignored. He has nightmares that Bruno takes over the entire team.

The players are like little kids getting away with something when the teacher's back is turned. They're almost silly. They don't notice the heat, the dirt, the sweat. They stop moaning about their tender elbows and sore knees, the muscle tweaks and kinks, all the symptoms of day-to-day play over a long season.

Bennie and Johnnie succeed on a hit and run play, but then botch a steal of home. Johnnie is out by three steps.

When they see that the younger guys aren't getting into trouble, the older players join the party. They're not noisy about it like the younger guys are. They're still not sure where this revolt will lead.

T.J. "forgets" to relay Skip's sign to the pitcher to throw over to first base to hold the runner. T.J. wants the runner to try to steal because he believes he can throw him out. Sure enough, the runner goes on the next pitch and T.J. nails him at second.

Skip never says a word about it.

Winston can't resist a hanging slider. He swings through another take sign and sends a solid single past the Pismo shortstop.

On a hit and run signal with Juan at first, Carlos lays down a bunt. It surprises everyone. The Inland Empire defenders were playing at double-play depth, hoping for a sharp grounder. Juan makes it to second and Carlos is safe at first.

When the Bears return home, the diehards—the fans who come to almost every game—figure out what's going on. They can see the disconnect. Although they can't read Coach's signs, they can tell that players aren't paying attention to him.

Word spreads as the Bakersfield Blaze comes to town. The stands are full. Everyone has an opinion.

"Cool."

"Way cool."

"Too much."

Most of the fans are in favor of the player takeover. Players on the Blaze aren't so sure.

"Silly."

"Stupid."

"What's the point?"

After the game, the Bakersfield skipper approaches Skip. Josh Burnett is an old-school manager, a strict disciplinarian.

"What's goin' on?" he inquires.

Skip shrugs and smiles.

"You gonna put up with this?" Burnett huffs. "It'll hurt the game. We'll all pay the price."

Skip puts his hands in the air and shakes his head, still smiling, and turns back to his own dugout.

Bennie is caught up in the rush of the rebellion. He's proud to feel that the other players are supporting him. On the other hand, he feels totally out of his depth, hardly able to stay afloat in all the excitement and confusion.

"Don't put it on me," he tells a TV reporter.

But in the public mind Bennie is the leader. A column appears on the sports page of the Union, the local newspaper.

Mutiny on the Diamond?
BY STEVE FARLEY

Is it a player revolt? Or isn't it? It depends on who you talk to this week at the Sierra Bears.

Whatever you call it, it's a very unusual occurrence in organized sports. The players have rebelled against management authority. They are ignoring orders and playing the way they want to.

And management is letting them. What choice do they have? Unless they're willing to forfeit games, they can't bench all the players who are disobeying them.

No one on the team will admit to any problems.

"There's no us and them," declares young Bennie Bruno, the trickster hitter whose unusual style is a favorite with fans. "It's only us. We all want the Bears to win."

"We're trying out a few new ideas," said Manager Skip Becker. "Everything's under control."

Is it? A few fans are concerned.

"The players are swingin' when they want and runnin' when they want," one Grass Valley man said, "Anybody can see it."

"They're blowin' it," said another. "No good can come from this."

"They were doing fine. Why change things?" a Nevada City mom complained.

One thing is sure and that's that the Bears are still winning. As long as that's the case, most folks aren't too worried about whether there's an uprising among the players or not.

The crowds grow. Everyone in town is tuned in. They feel personally involved with the Bears. It's like having thousands of aunts and uncles who feel it's their duty to offer advice about how to run your life.

Coach and Skip often eat breakfast together at Beefeaters when the team is back in Grass Valley. They're home-grown celebrities and the local potbellies drop by the table to shake hands with their very own public figures. It gets so they hardly have time to eat.

"Hey, Skipper, that new boy sure is stirrin' things up."

"How long you gonna put up with that nonsense?"

"You ought to show them who's the boss, Skip."

"Way to put those opposing teams off-balance."

The two Bears don't agree or disagree with anything they hear. They listen politely and grin in answer. Van Vranken has one iron-clad rule: don't get into it with the fan base.

Coach stops standing at the rail with the manager. Now he sits on the bench and there's a space around him where no one else goes. He's hard to be near these days. He seems old. He yawns a lot. He shows his stress in the set of his shoulders.

In baseball, nothing stays the same. There are hints of trouble, rocks in the road, easy to ignore.

The players are so elated with their new-found freedoms on the field that they decide to take some new freedoms off the field. There is more partying.

Except for Bennie, of course. But even he is guilty of less conditioning, less preparation for the team the Bears will face for the next game.

There are more errors. Guys too lazy to take that extra step. Too tired.

The running attack goes goofy. The guys run into stupid outs, not even sliding, just letting the opposing fielder slap a tag on them.

Reporters are buzzing around the team all the time now, as the season draws toward a close. Bennie seems to be the one pestered the most by requests for press interviews and autographs, by offers to make some extra money by doing a TV spot for a local car dealer or an air conditioning service or a barbeque restaurant. Could you find time to visit the sick children at the hospital? They're all big Bears fans. Would you allow us to auction a date with you to raise money for our community agency?

The stands are lined with fans before the game starts and Bennie signs their shirts and cards and caps until his hand aches. Being so young, it's hard for him to refuse.

He finds that his days fill up, cutting into the time he needs to get ready. He feels his energy diffuse. He loses focus. The whole team does.

Pretty soon, the entire Bears game is sideways. They're still winning, but it's not pretty. The team doesn't really deserve some of those W's.

Coach figures it's Bruno, taking the other guys out of their games. They should know better. They're all pros, men who have worked hard to get where they are. But the rook makes it look so easy to play a different way and, when they try it, they lose their rhythm.

Johnnie is totally juiced about the kid. They've become good friends. He digs the rook's aggressive defense. It fits his hot-blooded temperament. He doesn't like to wait for anything.

But lately he's been trying to mimic the rook's batting style. He pushes his hand up on the bat and tries to squib everything, only he's not any good at it. His average is way down in the last two weeks.

Pedro is trying to go small too. He says it gives his game an "unexpected element." Where did he pick up junk like that? Pedro is one of the Bears' big bats. He's supposed to go big, not small. He already strikes out too much. Now he's whiffing even more.

There's a game when Juan is on third and the rook comes up to bat. Coach is behind third, dancing around, his hands flying as usual.

Cap ear cap ear cap chin nose chin. Clap, Clap.

But it's like he's talking to himself in sign language because the rook's not even looking at him. When Bruno's at bat or aboard, Coach's signals are useless. Other players at least glance at him, flopping his hands over there at third. The looks might be habit and what they see may be only advisory, whereas before it was the law, but at least they look.

Not Bruno. No one on base has any clue what's going to happen or where the ball's going to go when he's at the plate. Runners can't run because the ball could be coming where they're going. It's every man for himself.

Bruno hits one of his twisty balls. Halfway toward third, it jigs to the right. The third baseman has no idea what to do and neither does Juan. He's afraid to leave the bag and Coach doesn't know what to instruct him to do.

Even though the kid makes it to first, Juan can't score. It makes him really sore.

The Bears depend on Juan, their number three batter, to get a lot of hits and plate a lot of runs. When he gets jangled, he can't do either one—score or hit—and the team is really hurting.

Bruno is a communications crisis on legs, as far as Coach is concerned. He's the cause of everything wrong with the team.

As the Bears stumble, the guys start to hassle each other in the clubhouse and even on the field.

They take sides about Bruno. What else?

To Johnnie, the rook can do no wrong.

Juan stays miffed because of the confusion on the bases.

The pitchers like the kid because he puts the other teams off-balance.

Devon, one of the first players to join the rebellion against management authority, decides he's in the anti-Bruno camp. He feels like Bennie shows him up on the field.

The whole controversy is bad news for the team.

Rancho Cucamonga comes to town for a three-game set. The Quakes are coming on strong and they throw their young phenom against the Bears.

Ken Sato was called up in June and he already has nine wins. He was drafted straight out of UCLA after he led the team to a victory in the College World Series. The Bears were fortunate to miss his turn in the pitching rotation the last time they faced Rancho Cucamonga.

Sato has his way with the boys the first and second times through the line-up. On his second at-bat, Johnnie lasts ten pitches before he hits a weak grounder to first. The rest go meekly, six strikeouts and ten infield outs, with one exception—Bruno.

Sato is super-careful of the kid. He walks him his first two times at bat. The second time, Bruno steals second. He gets to his feet, dusts himself off, touches the brim of his hat with his finger and points it at Sato.

"Damn you, Bennie," the pitcher says.

They know each other? Coach and Skip share a look. That's the first anybody on the Bears knew about it.

In the eighth inning, the Bears trailing 6-0, Bennie comes up with two outs and Devon on first. Sato starts him out with another wide one. On the next pitch—again well outside—Bruno leans far over the plate and barely manages to reach the ball. He sends a perfectly directed grounder between first and second. He holds up at first and Devon makes it all the way to third.

He steals second on Sato's first pitch to Winston, the next batter.

The pitcher walks around the mound, scowling at Bruno, clearly upset. They may be acquainted, Coach observes, but they're certainly not friends. In fact, Sato seems to dislike the rook.

Sato shakes off a couple signs from the Quakes catcher and then throws a fat one over the middle. Winston tees off on a line drive to left field.

Bennie catches up to Devon as they race down the line. He's two steps behind his teammate. The Quakes leftfielder gets the ball on one bounce and hurls toward home. As Devon slides safely across the plate, the catcher grabs the ball and slaps a tag on Bennie.

Out! Inning over.

The Quakes run off the field as Devon stands in front of Bennie.

"Way to go, hotshot. Way to kill the rally."

Sato finishes with 12 strikeouts. He dominates the Bears, except for Bennie. The Grass Valley squad loses 7-1.

Then comes the pile-up. Just when it seems like the Bears will always win, no matter what goes on in the clubhouse. Just when a California League Championship seems assured. Just when the Bears are the buzz of MILB.com . . . .

Their luck turns, just a little. That's all it takes. Like every streak, theirs wanes.

When they're on defense, seeing-eye grounders find the seams in the infield for hits. Easy bounces become too-hot-to-handle. Short hops don't come up, but skid under their gloves.

Two or three of those and the team loses a close game.

It happens to everybody on the squad. It's like measles. It's catching … that is, *not* catching … contagious.

When the Bears are at bat, blind-luck grounders find their way into opposing fielders' gloves, often raised only in self-defense. Bunts become pop-ups. Even for Bennie.

Bruno tries to counter the bad bounces with perfect placements on every hit ball. His strikeouts go up. His on-base percentage goes down.

Trying times. Trying too hard. Hard on everyone.

The Bears lose the Quakes series. The Bears lose a long road trip, dropping more games than they win. The Bears can't seem to get that big hit, the one with men on base. The relievers can't hold a lead.

A baseball hit high in the air and just starting to fall—that's what it feels like. The Bears are still the team to beat, but they're struggling.

The lead narrows. The Bears are four games ahead with 11 to go. What had seemed a sure thing is now in doubt. As they move into the final two weeks of the regular season, every game becomes crucial. There are no more who-cares losses.

As long as the Bears were winning, Skip didn't do anything. Now he moves swiftly.

"OK, Micah," he says, his hand on Coach's shoulder as they both stand at the dugout rail. "Time to resume command."

As Bennie comes to bat in a home game against Modesto, Coach gives him the take sign: *Chin ear chin ear chin nose cap nose.* Clap, clap.

Bennie ignores it and bunts at a high fastball. He hits it foul. Skip pops out of the dugout and pulls Bennie out of the game in the middle of his at-bat. The sub comes up with a one-strike count.

Two innings later, the Bears are behind by a run. Johnnie takes off from first on his own and steals a base, putting himself in scoring position. But Coach calls time and strides out to second. He yanks Johnnie, right there in front of all the fans. He puts in a pinch-runner, who finishes the game and plays third.

Pedro tries some smallball. With the bases empty in the seventh, he dismisses Coach's hand-signal and lays down a bunt. As he lumbers toward first, the Nuts catcher takes his time getting to the ball. He doesn't have to hurry. He throws Pedro out easily.

"Why did you do that?" Skip says as the big first baseman trots back to the bench.

"'Cause I wanted to," Pedro answers, brushing past his manager.

Skip watches Pedro go and then makes sure he keeps going. He trades him to Modesto that evening in return for their center-fielder, Eddie Briseño, a smaller and faster man who rarely strikes out. He moves Carlos to first base.

When the team shows up the next day, Pedro is gone. He never even had a chance to say goodbye. Briseño is unpacking into Pedro's old locker.

SLAM! The revolt is over. It's like shutting a door. It happens that quickly. It takes two benchings and one trade. One game.

Maybe Skip knows what he's doing after all.

The players are stunned. Nobody else challenges Coach. Nobody ignores his signs any longer. Everybody is afraid to be embarrassed. Or worse.

The guys fall in line quietly. Everybody has to behave himself. Even Bennie. He can't turn his back on the rest of the team now, not after the guys put it on the line to support him.

Coach schedules a batting session with him.

"Boy, you've got to get back to basics," he says. "You're gonna learn to keep that hand down."

"Coach, I can't ..."

"Yes, you can, son. At the very least, you can do your best."

"But . . . ."

"At the very least," Coach insists. "For the Bears."

Not exactly deep, two-way discussion, but Coach figures he earned the right to have it his way by waving his arms like a windmill for the last two weeks while the guys looked the other way.

But the Bears don't do any better. They drop two games out of three on a weekend series in Stockton. Eight to go. They're two and a half games ahead.

"Extra hitting drills," Coach declares. "Extra infield."

It doesn't do any good.

He and the Skipper try everything to get the guys back on track. They cancel infield. They hold extra batting practice. They skip BP.

None of it works.

"It's all about staying together," Coach says.

Skip puts in more running plays. Bennie strictly obeys the hand signals, but it doesn't matter. It doesn't help. Skip takes out the running plays.

Devon and Juan get into a mix-up before one game and then spend nine innings in the outfield trying not to look at each other.

Johnnie is irked by his teammates' sloppy play. He takes a two-hour shower so that everyone will be gone when he comes out. That way he won't lose his temper.

Coach puts a stop to the smallball. He signals for hits in the air.

Cap chin ear chin cap nose cap nose. Clap, Clap.

He signals for situational at-bats. A take to make room for a steal. A ball to the right side to move a runner over.

Chin ear chin ear chin nose cap nose. Clap, Clap.

He never flashes a bunt sign. He shuts down Bennie's catalog of little infield crazies.

The Bears lose a couple more close ones, games they should've won if they hadn't made blunders in the field. Johnnie hurries a throw across the diamond to first and Frankie can't dig it out of the dirt. Rizzo drops a routine fly to left.

For the first time, they hear a few boos from the fans. That makes the guys feel pretty low. It's bad enough to hit a hard stretch without having your fans turn on you.

There are more hassles in the clubhouse. Frankie gets on Johnnie, which is always a mistake. Devon backs him up. T.J. won't take sides.

"We're playin' like crap," the team captain says. "That about sums it up."

Then Carlos comes in with his hammie popped. He'd been working out with the rook, running up the steps, even though Coach told him not to. That routine was too much for Carlos. Now he's sitting on the bench, sulking, not helping the Bears one bit.

With Carlos down, Skip puts Richie Dean at first. Richie is on the team for his bat—occasionally big—not for his defensive skills. He can't get to as many balls as Carlos did and he's not as deft with the glove.

Bruno tries to take up the slack, covering a little more ground at second. Maybe he feels guilty because he's the one who screwed up Carlos.

"I should've been playing over more," he says, when Richie muffs a grounder to his right. "I can reach that ball."

He tries to take over the right side of the infield, cutting off balls to first whenever he can so that Richie doesn't have to make as many plays. The problem is that Bruno leaves the middle of the infield open, causing Devon at short to expand his range too.

Bruno's efforts backfire. Instead of cutting down on team errors, he increases them. He mixes up the infielders, causing more sloppy play, would-be outs turned into damaging hits. And that causes resentment.

"Stay away," says Richie. "I don't need you doing my job."

On an off-day for the Bears, the Quakes win both ends of a double-header, advancing to one and a half games behind. Sato throws a shutout in the second game.

Five games to play.

Skipper and Coach juggle the batting order, moving Eddie, the new centerfielder, to the second spot to take advantage of his speed. Richie moves to sixth.

No luck. The Bears lose another one. But so do the Quakes.

Next game Bruno and Devon get into it in the dugout between innings. When Bruno sits down next to him, Devon gets up and moves to the other end of the bench. Bruno watches him and then follows.

"What was that all about?"

"I don't want to be anywhere near you," Devon says. "You're stinking up the place."

"Get out of my face," the kid replies.

Devon stands and shoves the rook away. Bruno moves to confront him and finds his arms pinned from behind. He looks around to see who's doing it. It's Coach.

Devon snorts in Bruno's face and sits back down. The kid goes back to the other end of the dugout.

"Stop trying to take over the team," Coach tells him.

"Stay within yourself," Skip tells him.

Next inning, after another athletic defensive play at second, Bennie is trying to catch his breath when he comes up to bat. He's not settled in the batter's box and the first pitch comes inside and hits him on the little finger of his right hand.

It really hurts. He hops around and shakes his finger. Skip looks at it and decides it's not broken.

Bruno refuses to come out of the game. He trots to first and goes back on defense at the end of the inning.

With a runner at first, the batter hits a double play grounder to Devon at short. Bruno moves to second to take the throw, but Devon feeds him a ball that's low and late. Bruno has to lean over to catch it with his injured hand—a stinger to that tender finger—and then throw to first right away. He has no chance to move off the bag to get out of the way of the approaching runner, who slides and spikes Bennie's ankle.

OUCH!!

Bennie goes down hard. He has never felt pain like this before. It makes him sick to his stomach. It comes in waves pulsing down the side of his foot. He's sure his baseball days are over. He'll never play again, he's certain, and the pain will never end.

And then it does and he discovers he's lying on his side with both hands wrapped around his ankle. Smitty is next to him, murmuring, "Take it easy, just take it easy."

Bennie carefully rolls onto his knees and tries to pick himself up. Smitty has his arm around him as he puts his weight on that leg and—YOW!—he goes down again. Not good. Not good at all.

Smitty gestures for help. Devon and Frankie, one on each side, pick up Bennie in a seated position and shuffle off the field.

"I didn't do it on purpose, man," Devon says.

"I know you didn't. I didn't think that."

After the game, there's a phone call for Skip. The A's are calling up Johnnie. They're deaf to Skip's pleas to delay the move for a few days.

"We've got a weekend series with the Yankees," Billy Beane says. "We need him now."

Bennie or Johnnie—it's hard to say which loss hurts the Bears more.

Three games to go and the Bears are ahead by one.

The Bears close the season at home with a series against the Storm. The second-place Quakes finish with three against the Inland Empire 66ers.

Grass Valley goes electric. The little town never had a winner before. The fans are excited. They talk about the team in every coffee shop and corner café across the Sierras. There's a lot of concern about the Bears' poor play in the last couple weeks.

Fans overflow the stands. Van Vranken decides to amp up the crowd by hiring a cheerleader. He locates Marcie Doyle, a 19-year-old college student, and he dresses her up in a scanty costume as Goldilocks.

He gets three bear costumes in different sizes and he holds special contests before the game to find out who will wear them. Poppa Bear is the guy who wins a two-lap race around the infield. Momma Bear is the woman who hits the farthest ball in three swings. Coach agrees to soft-toss the pitches. And Baby Bear is the kid with the best growl.

Goldie is the judge. She's a big hit. The three bears, not so much.

The Bears win the opener behind a beautiful pitching performance from Robbie. Devon hits a two-run homer in the bottom of the eighth to ice the Storm.

The Quakes drop a close one to Inland Empire. The Bears are two up with two to go.

The fans, the mascots and Goldilocks all go crazy. Things are looking great. The team's fate is in the players' hands. All they have to do is win one more game and it won't make any difference what happens to the Quakes.

But that is not to be. The Quakes crush the Inland Empire on Saturday.

The Bears are an embarrassment. Carlos drops a long fly to center. Devon muffs an easy grounder to short. Mattie gives up seven runs in the first two innings.

"We look like Little League," Skip shouts afterward in the clubhouse. Skip never shouts. Ever.

"You want to win? Do you still want to win?" Coach challenges. "It doesn't show, if you do."

The mood is somber for the final regular season game. It feels like the slide will never end. The Bears have a one-game edge in the standings. Can they get it together one more time? Can they pick themselves up off the floor?

That Sunday afternoon, the team is like a broken record. Eighteen outs in a row to start the game. Two errors at second for Frankie. Bennie watches from the dugout, his ankle heavily taped.

Abe Emery gives up five runs in the first two innings. It's a downpour, a drenching from the Storm.

As T.J. steps to the plate for the fourth time in the eighth inning, a final score blinks in lights on the big scoreboard in the outfield. Down south, the Quakes defeated the Inland Empire.

That means the Bears need a win to take the league title. They need to rally, to show they can still win.

There are moans from the stands. The fans understand.

The Bears go quietly. At the end of the game—after Devon lofts an easy fly to left—there are a few cheers.

A few more boos, too.

The Bears back into a tie. A one-game playoff will decide the California League Championship.

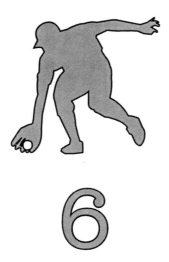

6

THE HALLS GET SMALL. The ceilings get low. Even for Bennie, certainly not the tallest boy in eighth grade.

Bayshore School is dumpy, dirty and dingy. The walls are stained. The rest rooms are shameful. How could he not have noticed it before?

At 14, he feels like he's too old for this place. The fifth and sixth graders squeal and laugh on the upper playground and the lower yard. He steps around them like they're some sort of pests, like noisy little rodents. The crayon drawings on display, the commotion in the lunchroom—all almost insulting, all juvenile. They're beneath Bennie now.

He feels like he's been at the same school for so long, too long, that he's become a fixture like one of those too-short water fountains no one uses. He finds himself giving directions to new teachers. He can't wait to get out of there.

The World Series is over and it's football season. The Niners play at Candlestick Park, just on the other side of the freeway less than a mile from the school. Ken is talking first downs and completed passes, blitzes and sacks, like most kids. But Bennie thinks of football as a distraction from his primary focus, which is… (all together now) … baseball.

He manages to turn most conversations back to his favorite sport.

"Algebra. I bet you can use it for hitting."

"That kid is a real curve ball."

"What would A-Rod do?"

"Bennie, please," Ken says. "It's almost Thanksgiving."

It's impossible for Bennie and Ken to spend as much time together during the school year as they do over the summer. Even though they're in the same grade, they're in different classrooms most of the time.

At lunch, they often sit together, joking and sharing stories. Sometimes Ken sits with the top-of-the-hill crowd. Sometimes he sits with Bennie *and* the top-of-the-hill crowd, which causes an interesting tension at the table and a lot less joking on Bennie's part. He feels tolerated, like a pet turtle.

"They allowin' you to sit at their table?" Franklin taunts Bennie. "You gonna get too uppity for us flatlanders?" He laughs.

To avoid the awkwardness, Bennie starts to take his lunch and sit with Ray in his little room off the hallway. Nobody else goes there.

"Hey, Bennie. How's it goin'?"

Ray welcomes the company. He's a baseball-only fan like Bennie and he never tires of talking about the Giants. He wears a Giants shirt, jacket and hat year-round.

After school, there's intramural volleyball or inter-school basketball. Ken joins the teams because he enjoys organized activities. A social animal, he likes going to the other middle schools.

If it isn't baseball, Bennie avoids it.

Bennie and Ken still spend a couple afternoons a week together. They play what they call Faraway. They start playing catch and then back up one step after every throw. Pretty soon, they're far apart, throwing with all their might. It helps strengthen Ken's pitching arm. It makes Bennie's outfield throws more accurate. That ends when the winter rains kick in.

Ken tutors Bennie in PlayStation and in Wii. Baseball, of course, but also racing and war games. The shortest reaction time wins. They learn to think fast, to make quick decisions. Bennie figures this will help him as both a batter and a fielder.

The boys continue their ping pong. It's the one game, besides baseball, where Bennie has a chance against Ken. They play entirely different styles.

Ken has his spectacular slam game. His aim is annihilation. He tries to take advantage of his growing height advantage, putting Bennie on the defensive so that he's reacting instead of attacking.

Bennie is a finesse player, relying on deft drops over the net or corner shots. He's cutting his shots now, slicing his paddle across the ball instead of hitting it squarely. The result is that the ball veers in one direction or the other when it hits on the other side of the net.

Ken has to charge and stretch to make awkward returns. Bennie gets some rare opportunities for slams of his own.

Bennie chops a particularly nasty spin. The ball lands and skims to the side and off the table.

"What if you could do that to a baseball?" he wonders.

"No way," Ken pants. "Not to a 90 mile-per-hour fast ball."

A rousing conclusion. A 10-hit volley, including two slam returns by Bennie and one off-the-side save by Ken. Ken's point.

"You've gotten better," Ken tells his friend. "A lot better."

Ken comes by the Bruno apartment once while Bennie drops off his backpack. Mike isn't there, but Sarah Ann makes the visit memorable when she walks in on the two boys in the kitchen. Just out of the shower, she's blow-drying her hair, a bath towel barely containing her bigger-by-the-week boobs.

"I'm Ken," Ken says, stepping forward and offering his hand.

"Oh, that's sweet," Sarah Ann says. "You can call me Impressed. And stop looking at my chest." Which is, of course, exactly what she wants him to do.

Ken colors. The boys hurry out.

Deep dusk and Bennie is alone on the little field at the top of the hill. The fog is in and it's chilly. The grass is still damp from the rain that afternoon, but he doesn't notice. He's focused on his bunting. He can do that on his own.

Bennie tosses the ball up, slides both hands onto the bat and shoves the ball forward. How high should he bring the upper hand? He experiments with different distances between his two hands.

The field is uneven, so sometimes it's tough to tell what the ball is doing. It's deflected by clumps of weeds and gopher holes. But sometimes it seems that the ball skips to the side. Bennie tries to figure out what makes the ball act like that. He discovers that it happens when he skids the bat across the ball, sort of a slicing motion like he uses in ping pong. If he hits the ball head-on, it tends to go straight.

He's never seen anyone do that before. It's difficult because the ball is wet and slippery, but he keeps trying to duplicate that slice that makes the ball bounce sideways.

He's concentrating so hard, honing in, that he doesn't realize it's full dark until he loses the ball. He only hit it about 10 feet in front of him, but he can't see it. He searches the area until he kicks the ball and then he picks it up.

He gathers his glove and bat. He looks around him. The sky is full of stars and a slice of moon.

He has nowhere else to go. Mike has his football buddies over for the Monday night beer and cheer. The plastic curtain to Bennie's alcove doesn't keep the sound out. It will be noisier than usual tonight. It's never quiet, never private. It's never a good place for homework.

Sarah Ann has decided she will only answer to S-A. "Because it's cool," she explains, fingering the black skull she had tattooed on her ear lobe. S-A is entertaining a couple girl friends. There's definitely no place for Bennie in her room.

"Why aren't you home," Ma complains all the time. "You're always gone I don't know where."

"Should I bring my friends home so we can sit under the table?" Bennie answers.

Ma works late on Mondays, her way of avoiding the weekly football bash.

Up at the top of the hill, most of the houses have Christmas decorations. Nobody can afford to spend money on colored lights down in the flats, except for PG&E. The giant utility strings colored lights on its antenna farm as if the towering metallic spires were happy holiday trees.

Bennie doesn't spend evenings with Ken because the Satos consider after supper to be homework time. But he drifts in that direction, just killing time before he has to face the clatter and clutter at his own apartment.

He rounds the corner in time to see a cab pull up outside the Sato house. An older Japanese man gets out and reaches back for a couple bulging suitcases. Ken and his parents come to the door. Mrs. Sato comes down the sidewalk and Bennie can overhear her greeting.

"Tatsuo. What a surprise."

"I have come to America."

"So you have."

An enthusiastic embrace. Ken's father arrives to struggle with one of the bulging suitcases. Tatsuo hefts the second one with no apparent effort and limps up the walk.

Ken notices Bennie and waves.

Bennie gets the key from the pot by the rosebush and lets himself into the house through the garage. He's there to feed Andy, the terrier, as he always does when Satos are out of town for the weekend. He plans to practice a little ping pong while he's here.

He goes to the family room and—whoops! The ping pong table is folded up and pushed against the wall. The uncle is there. He looks up in surprise and rises from a mat on the floor.

"I'm sorry," Bennie begins. "I didn't know you were in here."

"Not problem," the older man says. He speaks English slowly, like he's translating everything in his head.

"I forgot you were here, Mister … Mister …" Bennie realizes he doesn't know the man's last name. He heard Mrs. Sato call him Tatsuo, but he assumes that's a first name.

"Call me Unk," the older man says and offers his hand to shake.

"Hi. I'm Bennie." He shakes Unk's hand. "I was going to feed Andy. I feed him when Satos go out of town."

"Andy already fed."

"Ah, well, I won't bother you. I'll be going." Bennie is embarrassed.

"You baseball player," Ken's uncle says, pointing to Bennie's glove, which is hooked around his belt. Bennie rarely goes anywhere without his glove.

"That's right," Bennie says, backing out of the room.

"December?" the older man asks.

"Uh-huh," Bennie says, totally clueless. "New Years Week. No school."

The uncle smiles and points again to Bennie's glove.

"Basketball?" he asks.

"No, baseball." Bennie takes a ball from his back jeans pocket. Unk shakes his head.

"No. Please excuse bad speaking. What mean, is December. Why not basketball?"

"Oh. I'm just a baseball guy, " Bennie says. "That's my sport."

Unk nods. He takes the baseball and flips it in the air and catches it with one hand. Then he flips it back to Bennie and smiles.

"Good meet you, Mr. Bennie."

When Ken gets back, Bennie tells him about the conversation with Unk.

"Yeah, he played for the Swallows in Tokyo," Ken says. "Four years until he hurt his knee."

"Is that their major leagues?"

"Oh, yeah. NPB. Nippon Professional Baseball. Uncle Tatsuo used to be quite an athlete."

As the weeks wear on, wet and wetter, Bennie puts away his glove. He moves through the late winter days bored, depressed, deprived of his only real love.

One afternoon, Bennie, Ken and Jeffrey are lolling around the Sato house.

Jeffrey Fong is new to the Bayshore. His family lives about four doors down from Satos. A nice guy, never pushy, he's been spending a lot of time with Ken.

Unk wanders into the room. He's wearing a long-sleeved tee shirt and gray sweatpants.

"Not nice weather," he says.

"Guess we need the rain," Ken answers glumly.

"Want play baseball?" Unk asks.

"I wish," Bennie says.

"Maybe not games, but good time learn special skills," Unk says. "Help play better baseball."

"What kind of skills," Jeffrey asks.

"Probably karate," Ken quips. He goes into a frozen karate position, a crane with one leg in the air, like the kid did in the movie.

Everyone laughs, even Unk. He holds his finger up to his eye.

"Eye openers," he says and grins.

So the three Bayshore boys, with nothing better to do, agree to try some Tokyo baseball drills. They meet after school to work with the former Japanese pro.

"Exercises make better sight," Unk says.

He gives Ken a pencil and motions for him to hold it at arm's length.

"Focus on number on side of pencil," Unk says. "Now bring toward you—slow—until number start blur."

Ken brings the pencil closer to his face and then pauses.

"Do again," Unk orders.

Ken does. Unk gives him a second pencil.

"Hold one far away and hold other close so numbers not blurring," he says.

Ken gets the two pencils lined up.

"Now," Unk says. "Focus on closer one and then focus on farther one. Nearer, farther. Nearer, farther."

Ken is moving his eyes back and forth.

"Be sure focus," Unk says. "Now do five minutes."

Ken is blinking and rubbing his eyes by the time he's done. Unk gives the pencils to Bennie and gives two more to Jeffrey. Pretty soon they're all blinking.

"Good," Unk says after a brief break. "Now do again. Doing push-ups with eyes. How useful for baseball?"

"Hitting," Bennie says.

"Right," Unk says. "To hit ball, must see ball. "

He takes a white Wiffle ball and he writes numbers on the different planes, using a colored marker. Then he ties a string around the ball and hangs it from the ceiling. He positions Jeffrey beneath the ball and then twirls it.

"Read numbers," Unk says.

Jeffrey recites: "Seven—one—nine—one—four—six—nine—seven."

Each has a turn. All three are rubbing their eyes in a few minutes.

"This help concentrate," Unk says. He twirls the ball faster.

"Faster better. Baseball very fast game," he says.

The purpose of the eye exercises, he tells the boys, is to "slow game." He bows to them.

"That all today."

The next day they meet in Ken's garage. Unk has cleared an area in the back and chalked a square about the size of a strike zone on the back wall. He puts a small board on the floor to represent home plate. He puts a small, narrow board under the opened garage door to represent the rubber.

"Kenny. Stand at plate."

Unk takes a baseball and colors it between the seams—blue, red, green, yellow. Then he stands on the rubber and throws the ball at the back wall.

"Curve ball," he says as the first pitch crosses the plate. "What colors you see?"

"Blue and green and red, I think," Ken answers.

"Correct," Unk says. "Ball spinning make curve, so see different colors."

He throws a second pitch. It hits low on the chalk strike zone.

"Fast ball," Unk says. "What colors?"

"Red and a little yellow," Ken says.

"Ball spin less," Unk says. He throws a third pitch. It bounces on the wooden plate.

"Change up."

"Green and blue," Ken says.

As Unk continues to throw, each of the boys takes his turn standing at the plate. They don't swing a bat, not a real one, anyways. Sometimes, they swing an air bat. But mostly they're just trying to identify each pitch.

"Change up," Jeffrey says.

"Curve," Unk says. "Don't guess. Say don't know."

"This is hard," Jeffrey complains. "I can't see the ball against the glare from outside."

"Happen in real game," Unk says. "Sun shines on outfield. Pitcher in glare throw to batter in shadow."

So it goes. It takes several days before the boys can consistently call the pitches.

"Spin key," Unk says. "Need see spin to hit ball."

The rain lets up. The batting cages open. The boys brave the long bus ride down to Redwood City one Saturday in March. Bennie has some money he's been saving since Christmas. The pitching machines eat quarters like a downtown parking meter.

Because of Unk, the boys have been thinking and talking about baseball for weeks. They've been practicing their seeing at every opportunity. To their surprise, the balls shout off their bats.

"Yow," Ken calls. "This is easy."

"This is fun," Jeffrey calls from the neighboring cage.

Bennie says, "The balls are just floating in."

They set up a friendly competition. They put the machine on "fast." For each 20-pitch cycle, they keep track of misses (minus one), hits (plus one) and balls that make it to the back screen in the air (plus two).

Bennie and Ken are neck and neck most of the way. Jeffrey hits mostly grounders.

"Timing. It's all about the timing," Ken says.

He and Bennie tie with top scores of 14 (for one cycle) before the contest is called on account of coins. Even Jeffrey and Ken run out of money.

Elated, eager to test their skills, the boys decide to find a game. On a sunny spring day the following week, they take the bus up Geneva and hop off when they see some people playing baseball. It's City College, a pickup game. The players are normal students, not the school team.

Ken has grown. He's pretty lanky for an eighth grader. He fields the question from a tall black kid.

"We're juniors at Jeff," Ken says.

Bennie and Jeffrey nod. They look a little short, but ready to play ball. Bennie is punching his mitt over and over.

"Oh, yeah? Ms. Robleda still there?" The black kid asks.

"Uh . . . ," Ken begins.

The black kid laughs and looks over at the other players. He opens one hand in question.

A stocky Filipino youth shrugs. "We could use a couple more. Put the two short ones in the outfield. I'll take the skinny kid."

The black kid jerks his thumb toward the outfield. Bennie and Jeffrey sprint onto the field and Ken trots toward the dugout. Bennie can't stop grinning as he takes his position in left.

What a fine field, all green and even. It's a long way to home plate, a lot further than their little field up on the hill. And the outfield stretches forever, all the way to the chest-high chain fence back by the road.

Bennie hears a crack, looks back and barely has time to protect his face with his glove. The ball bounces away toward the third base line. Flustered, he gives chase.

He reaches the ball at the base of the fence and turns around to see the runner rounding second. He hurls with all his might—it really is a long way to the infield—and the ball hits the ground ten feet shy of the infield. Those Faraway games really paid off.

But the strong throw surprises the shortstop, who bobbles the ball. The runner scores with no play at the plate. An inside-the-park home run.

Because of Bennie's error.

He goes to his position, flexes his legs and focuses on the next batter. The game is unforgiving. All he can do is do better.

There are no more incidents. The next three batters make outs on the infield. No one says anything when Bennie comes into the dugout and plops down next to Jeffrey. He shares a grimace with his friend. He feels like a piece of chewed gum stuck to the under-side of the wooden seat.

Jeffrey is up this inning. He hits the ball hard, but it goes straight to the third baseman.

It's Bennie's turn the following inning. The first pitch is in the dirt and he skips over it. He can see the ball clearly. He can tell that the pitcher is not a real pitcher, just someone trying to get the ball over the plate.

The second pitch is high. Bennie realizes the pitcher has no control and that he has an advantage, his height or lack of. He squats down, making himself even shorter.

The pitcher is a wiry young Latino. He seems to be only a couple years older than Bennie. The area where he's standing is only slightly elevated. The mound hasn't been built up yet.

Bennie calms down. He focuses. The next pitch comes in and it's called a strike on the outside corner. Bennie is never tempted.

The fourth pitch is outside. A count of 3 and 1. Bennie takes a deep breath.

The next pitch comes in like a pumpkin. As Bennie had hoped, the pitcher slows the ball down to make sure he gets it over the plate. Bennie tenses and waits and then puts a solid swing on it. The ball scoots under the pitcher's glove and into center field.

As he pulls up at first, Bennie spots Ken in the outfield, flashing him a quick thumbs-up. He's so pleased with his hit that the rest of the game is a blur.

He reaches second on a walk and a passed ball, but then grounds out his next time up.

Jeffrey catches a fly ball, but he doesn't hit anything. On his only time up, Ken takes a walk.

Then the game breaks up. There doesn't seem to be a signal or a reason.

"People got things to do," says the stocky Filipino, Raymond. "You guys OK? You did good."

"Thanks for letting us play," Ken says.

The boys walk back home. It's downhill and they're too amped to sit on the bus.

"I thought that black kid ... " Jeffrey begins.

"Isaac," Bennie interjects.

"I thought he was going to pound you into the ground like a spike," Jeffrey laughs.

"I thought he was going to ask me what that Ms. Robleda teaches," Ken chuckles. "I figured they all knew we weren't from Jeff."

"They all knew," Jeffrey and Bennie agree at the same time.

"Can you believe it?" Ken laughs.

High-fives all around. Almost out of middle school.

Jeffrey changes things. They were changing anyway, but Jeffrey speeds things up.

Both from Asian backgrounds, Jeffrey and Ken have a lot in common. Their parents put a lot of academic pressure on them and their traditional grandparents demand that they observe cultural holidays.

Both boys are smart and computer-savvy and they have money. Jeffrey joins Ken in the San Mateo League on Wednesday evenings and Saturday mornings. It cost a couple hundred dollars for the uniforms, equipment and umpires.

"You should've seen him," Jeffrey says, eager to share stories of Ken's successes. "The Sluggers send up this ringer. The guy had to be 18 at least. He was like seven feet tall."

The League is for 11 to 14-year-olds. Both boys are in their last year. They take to wearing their team shirts, the Cardinals.

"Ken blew it by him. The guy lifts the bat off his shoulder and— thwack!—the ball's in the catcher's mitt." Jeffrey is very proud of his friend. "He never had a chance."

"I could see he was slow," Ken says. "He moved like a building."

Lots of laughter. Lots of left-out for Bennie. He tries to be the attentive audience, but it hurts. While the Cardinals practice and compete, Bennie is by himself. He feels like the boy at the bottom of the hill, the very bottom, the boy who lives under the dining room table, the boy with nothing to do and no one to do it with.

But he gets over feeling sorry for himself pretty quickly. As the summer break begins, he decides he needs to search for more games where he can play.

"Let's go back to City," Bennie says. "Let's go back to Crocker."

"I dunno … " Jeffrey says. He and Ken are more into movies and computer games these days.

So Bennie gives it a go solo. He buses up Geneva, but he can't find any pickup games at City. He drives past on four different days.

He goes down to Crocker. Sure enough, neighborhood kids trickle into the park by mid-morning. By midday, there are usually enough people to put together teams.

Nobody knows Bennie, so he hangs out for a few days before anybody chooses him. He spends more days on the bench as fifth outfielder and backup catcher. He's the guy who warms up the pitcher between innings.

It's not much fun for him by himself. He can't connect with anyone. He doesn't feel like he's learning much.

Back to Bayshore, back to the wall behind the school. Bennie works on his fielding. He returns to the pocket park, the practice wall by the tennis court. The nets are up, so he stands close and gets in some more hours on those bunts.

Bennie assumes that Unk is with his nephew. He figures he's going to the league games and working with Ken afterward. But he's not. He's watching Bennie—sometimes from a distance, sometimes on his daily walks. He sees the boy trudging by himself, bat and glove over his shoulder. He sees a boy who loves baseball.

Unk had no intention of getting involved with baseball at any level ever again. He came to America to get away from *yakyu*, which is what the Japanese call baseball.

In Japan, Unk was famous and he's in constant pain because of it. He was a recognized name as a young man when he became the Swallows' starting second baseman. He came to America because he did *not* want to be a hard-luck has-been.

His knee trashed, his career over, he came to America to learn to live lean. Lean meaning without fat, without fans, without success, without excess. Without *yakyu*.

He came with the clothes on his back and what he could carry in two suitcases. Now he is just Unk. Not Tachi Tanaka, let alone Tachi-san, the figure on the 30-foot billboard by the bullet train.

Just Unk limping the hills of Daly City. Another anonymous Asian on the wrong side of the Pacific Ocean.

Just Unk laying low, staying slow, trying to get over it all.

But he is not free of his past. His reconstructed knee throbs with every step. His deconstructed life robs him of sleep.

And he can't help himself. He can't help noticing the way Bennie feels about baseball. He can't help responding to the boy's reverence for the game. It reminds him—of so many things, of himself when he was younger.

The next Wednesday evening, when he knows Bennie will be alone because the other boys are playing a league game, Unk stations himself near the apartments. He is not surprised to see Bennie coming down the sidewalk, a sandwich in one hand and his glove in the other.

"Play some baseball?" Unk asks.

"I wish," Bennie says, smiling because he gave the same answer the last time Unk asked the same question. "Eye openers?"

"Leg warmers." He does pretty well for a guy still learning the language. He reaches for the sandwich. "Save for you."

"But . . . ."

"Better eat later."

After pumping up the hill for the fourth time, Bennie is grateful he doesn't have a full stomach.

Unk is resting at the halfway point, sitting on the curb.

"Doing good, Mr. Bennie," he says. "Keep it up. Then keep it down." He chuckles.

Bennie reaches the top of the hill and pauses, his hands on his knees, while he catches his breath.

"Keep coming," Unk shouts. "Keep coming now, boy."

In some ways it's harder coming downhill. Bennie can feel it in his legs.

"What have to do with baseball?" Unk asks, as Bennie goes by.

Bennie is out of breath. "Don't know." Puff, puff.

"Yes you do,"

Puff, puff. "Stronger legs, I guess." Puff, puff.

"Can't hear, boy."

Bennie is getting to the bottom of the hill. He has to shout to be heard.

"Stronger legs," he yells. "Better wind."

"Good. Very good," Unk pats his back as Bennie labors past him again. "Sweat good, Mr. Bennie. Sweat your friend."

Seven times up, six plus coming down. They quit when Bennie's legs get wobbly. Unk grabs the boy by the arm and steadies him.

"In Japan, baseball very different for players," Unk explains. "Work much harder than America. Get in shape for game."

They walk back toward the apartments. Bennie wipes the sweat off his face with the back of his sleeve. He wolfs the rest of his sandwich. Unk disapproves.

"Taste what you eat," he says. "Teach body new ways to be happy."

Pepper.

The prospect of a black eye.

The possibility of a bloody nose.

"Why it called hardball," Unk says.

A baseball is small and fast and tricky and it hurts if it gets you before you get it.

"Being brave," Unk says. "Keeping eyes open."

The good ones aren't afraid. They're eager. They want the ball.

Catch the ball and get a point. Miss it, lose a point. Throw it and if the batter can't hit it, you lose a point. The game has a rhythm. Catch the ball throw the ball hit the ball catch the ball throw the ball.

Pepper.

The faster you go, the better.

But don't get a bad bounce. Don't play on an uneven surface. Slow ball fast ball grounder line drive.

"First lesson paying attention," Unk says.

Don't let the baseball bite. Pepper.

Bennie loves this game—the risk, the pace, the total immersion. You can't think of anything else when you're playing pepper. You can't do it halfway.

Saturday afternoon and the warm weather draws the boys outside. It's Bennie, Ken and Jeffrey. They're on the schoolyard because the asphalt provides an even playing surface.

Unk is the batter, hitting soft ones at first and then slapping stingers. The idea is to keep the ball in motion, to keep the game going.

Jeffrey catches one on his chin, an in-between hop he can't handle. The impact sits him on his butt.

"Come in on ball," Unk tells him.

Jeffrey rubs his chin. He picks up the ball and throws it back to Unk, who hits it right back at the boy. This time Jeffrey fields it cleanly.

Unk introduces another new game, one they can play on the uneven field at the top of the hill. Unk stands on the cardboard mound and tosses the ball, calling the field where the batter is supposed to hit it—right, left or center. The batter gets a point every time he hits to the correct field. The other players earn points by catching the flies. If the batter hits the ball to the wrong field or if he pops up on the infield, the players switch positions.

Pepper taught the boys how to play infield. Toss Up, as Unk calls it, teaches them to play outfield.

But the days when Ken and Jeffrey play get fewer and fewer. There are other things they'd rather do. A distance grows between Bennie and Ken. There are no dramatic breaks, nothing like that, but it's not quite what it was.

Unk tries to interest the three boys in running, always the running.

"Best thing for you," he insists.

He takes them to the hill and puts them through the same drill he did before with Bennie.

Jeffrey is miserable. Ken is red with effort, panting and suffering.

"What does this have to do with baseball?" he shouts.

"Tell him, Mr. Bennie."

"Stronger legs." Bennie chugs up the incline. "Better wind."

"It's boring," Ken says.

"It's no fun at all," Jeffrey adds.

"Work fun," Unk says from his perch halfway up.

"Maybe for you it is," Jeffrey comments, slowing to a walk as he comes down the grade.

Jeffrey creates friction between Bennie and Ken. He seems to go out of his way to disagree with Bennie, to create a dispute.

"Let's play this." Bennie suggests.

"Nah, let's play that," Jeffrey says. "What do you think, Ken?"

Everything is decided now by vote. Always 2-1. There's always a loser. Usually Bennie. What happened to the days when everybody won?

Ken and Jeffrey decide they won't run the hill any more. They get into skateboarding. Bennie tries a few times, but he can't afford to buy the board. Unk opposes the sport, claiming it can lead to injuries.

"Any sport can," Jeffrey says, rubbing a big bruise on his forearm where he "caught" a hot line drive.

Ken and Jeffrey get into water polo. Bennie can't get to the pool, can't pay the day fee.

So Unk takes Bennie back to the hill. Up and down a few times. Unk takes to timing him. Straining, gaining a few seconds on his earlier climbs.

Bennie builds up his legs. He builds up his lungs. He doesn't complain. He doesn't mind. Every step is a step closer to first base, to second base, to any base in Bennie's dream, the dream of Big League baseball.

It's not unusual for a teen to shy away from work, like Ken and Jeffrey. What's unusual is the kid like Bennie, ready to do anything for the sport. They say Einstein felt that way about numbers; they marched constantly through his mind. Bennie feels that way about baseball.

Ken enjoys a more balanced lifestyle. He excels at school. Why not? It's easy for him. He likes a lot of his studies. Science is interesting. English is involving. Math is challenging. Of course, he has little choice because his father watches him closely.

There's a price, it's true, for Bennie's immersion in baseball. His grades aren't good, but they aren't bad. He gets by, barely, because it's easier than getting into academic trouble.

All three boys are at the stage where their boyhood is nearly over, like it or not. They don't talk about it, but they know somehow.

They know that soon they'll be expected to act like adults. They'll have to account for their time. They'll have to be responsible, maybe even get jobs. They'll have more work at school.

They won't have these long days, these hours aching to be filled, sunshine the only way they tell time. They won't be able to be children any more.

There's a special quality to everything they do this summer, a fleeting feeling. Like tasting the last morsel. Like two outs in the bottom of the ninth.

MOST KIDS IN Daly City don't go to high school for love of learning. They don't attend because they want to get ahead and need a decent education. They go to DC High—DC, they call it—because they're required to go. They're supposed to spend their days off the streets, away from the world, crowding the concrete corridors and quads.

The long, low buildings all look alike. Narrow hallways packed with laughing cliques, couples in cling, clots of wide-bodied boys turned in on their private mischiefs. Shouts and whoops. Curses. The clamor of slamming lockers.

Droopy jeans, double-x shirts and pulled-down beanies, everything supersized, everything disguised—this is the uniform of the informed teen, male or female. DC doesn't have individuals. It has inmates, all dressed alike.

Nothing at all like middle school, DC is intense, enveloping, overwhelming. It can be forbidding to a freshman. Scary.

To Bennie, it feels like opportunity.

DC isn't the best academic school in the area, but it has the best athletic program. That's why Ken came here instead of Westlake, the better academic school about a mile away.

There's a weight room, a gym, a swimming pool. Fields of play. That's right, fields. One for football, one for soccer circled by a mile-long track, two for baseball. Two.

During the first semester, Bennie keeps busy staying in shape. He runs the stairs on the big bleachers. It's easy after the hill at Bayshore. He tries his hand at the weights. He swims to build up his arms. He doesn't sign up for any teams, but he often stays after school to use the facilities.

And not to go back to the apartment.

Mike and Ma are at each other hard and loud lately. Ma lost her job and she's home by herself most of the time. Everyone avoids her. Sarah Ann and Mike are rarely there.

"You'll be sorry," Sarah Ann says on her way out as Bennie comes home.

That's the nicest thing she's said to him in weeks.

Sarah Ann is the warrior queen of the household. She carries her attitude around like a lance, knocking over everything within five feet of her. She's using her whole name again, not just initials, all in capital letters.

Bennie's too big for her to boss around any more, but not too big to belittle. That's his sister's strategy: to cut her little brother down to size, to make fun of him, to keep him her inferior.

"Can't you stay out of my way? Didn't you hear what I said? What part of stupid don't you understand?"

If Bennie answers, she asks: "Are you talking to someone?"

It tends to keep the boy quiet. To keep him absent.

Sarah Ann has a boyfriend named Edgar or Edge, as he likes to be called. Edge plays right field for the DC varsity squad. Edge drives Sarah Ann to school every morning. He comes by in his big old clunker a few minutes before school begins.

Bennie is never invited. Ever.

At school, Sarah Ann is punky and painted. She's at the center of the social web, which is more important than anything else at DC to most of the inmates. Grades, awards, any kind of adult praise—none of it is as important as where you are on that web.

The strands of the web are social interactions. Each of them is super-sticky, spider-sticky, but there's no spider. Only flies, all stuck.

And Bennie? He's at the outer rim of the web. A freshman, he's almost unnoticed, except when his sister taunts him.

"Beanie! Hey, Beanie!" She calls across campus to him. When he was little, it was affectionate. Now the nickname is mean.

"Beanieeeeee! Oh, Beannnniieeeeee."

And then she leans against a wall or against Edge and laughs so hard, she's so pleased with herself.

"Cawcawcawcaw." She sounds like a crow.

Bennie hates it. He tries to stand up to her.

"Leave me alone, Sarah Ann. Pick on your own pimples," he sneers.

"What?" Sarah Ann shrills, looking around to be sure all her friends are watching. "You're bad-mouthin' ME?? I'll padlock the john, Beanie. I'll cut off your balls, BEANIE!"

All at the top of her lungs. All complete with bows and gestures to the audience, her gang. Bennie is pinned to the floor by the sheer volume of Sarah Ann's assault and by her cruel laughter.

"Cawcawcawcaw."

Baseball practice begins right after the first of the year. It starts with tryouts. The kids run drills inside the gym because it's raining outside. The noise is monstrous—sneakers skreeking on the hardwood, coaches yelling, all echoed by the empty seats.

They split into pairs and play catch, using tennis balls because the coaches don't want to damage the floor with hardballs. It reminds Bennie of his schoolyard game against the library wall.

Saturday is clear and the boys meet early in the morning on the muddy field. They can see their breaths as they warm up. It feels good to swing a bat. It feels good to be outside.

The boys are split into two groups. The coaches make lots of substitutions every inning, so they can see what each kid can do. Sometimes they tell a boy to play different positions.

That first day, everyone spends some time on his back or on his face. The field is that slippery. It's hard to run. It's even harder to stop.

Bennie slides into second and keeps going all the way into short centerfield. Covered in mud, he's tagged before he can get back to the bag and he can't stop laughing, even though he's out. He points at the opposing catcher. Great throw!

He can hardly contain himself, he's so pleased to be playing baseball. He laughs every time he falls down. He laughs every time someone else falls down. Bennie's so happy he's giddy.

He has such a good time, it's easy to overlook that some of the other boys are really struggling. More than 60 boys show up for tryouts. Twenty-five make the Rams varsity team, including 23 who played for Daly City High the previous year. Bennie and Ken are the only freshmen. Jeffrey makes the junior varsity, the freshman squad.

The four-month season starts in mid-February. There are real games with real teams. Nine boys on the field playing together.

Games that last nine innings. With umpires.

Bennie can't get enough. Games to show him what he can do and cannot (not yet). Games where he can (finally) find out how good he is.

Uniforms. Cap. Cleats. Bennie is blissed.

The weather turns better and the baseball diamond is groomed into immaculate condition. No bumps or clumps or stumps. Actual grass, soft and mown and grown just to play baseball. He wants to roll in it, it's so springy, so fine. It smells like sunlight.

It has chalk baselines and real bases and an actual pitcher's mound, elevated and exactly sixty feet, six inches from home plate. With a backstop.

The field is a wonderful thing to Bennie. He's often the last to leave. Coach Cortes has to shoo him off the field. He'd live there if they'd let him.

As good as he is, Bennie doesn't get a lot of extra attention from Coach Cortes or his assistant, Mr. Brattle. Coach teaches PE and health. Short and paunchy, he wears a baseball cap over his bald crown. A whistle hangs down over his belly. Mr. Brattle is a math teacher. He also has a whistle and he loves to blow it to show the boys he's important.

They're both more interested in Ken. They see his natural ability, his graceful moves. They see an ace, a number one starting pitcher, something that the Rams haven't had for years.

"Sato, I want you to throw a few to Mason," Coach says and watches closely. "Uh huh. OK, now let's see if you can hit his glove."

Tommy Mason, the senior catcher, holds his glove inside. Ken hits it. Outside. Ken hits it.

"Bounce one off the plate," Coach said. Ken does it.

Coach confers with Mr. Brattle.

"Can you throw a curve?" Brattle asks.

Ken throws a few. He's still not very accurate. "I was hoping you could help me on that," he says.

"I was hoping that very thing," Coach says.

While they work with Ken, Bennie has a chance to find his own way. He's pegged as a utility man, meaning he can play any position, but mostly the infield.

All those hours at the wall are finally paying off for Bennie. He has no fear of the ball. None at all. He knows to keep his head down, watch the ball into his glove. He can move from side-to-side quickly. His throws to first are fast and true.

"Where'd you learn to throw like that?" Oliver Wilson is the Rams first baseman, a junior.

"A game Unk showed me," Bennie says.

"Your uncle?" Oliver says. "I also am an uncle."

"Uhh, it's a long story," Bennie says.

"I walk all the way to BART," Oliver says.

"Yeah? I live in that direction."

"I know," Oliver says. "You can catch the 14 back to Bayshore from the corner."

"You're right," Bennie says. "How do you know that?"

Oliver just smiles. Bennie heists his backpack and falls in next to the large Pacific Islander youth.

"You're an uncle?"

Twice over, Oliver informs him. Not only that, but he lives with his two little nephews, his sister's kids, as well as his sister, his other sister, his granny, his nanny, his mammy, and his pa. All in a three-room apartment, sleeping in shifts.

"I like it out on the field," Oliver says. "Lots of room to move around."

"I hear that," Bennie says, thinking of his alcove in the dining room.

Oliver is talkative and observant. He becomes an invaluable ally to Bennie.

"Just work hard," Oliver says. "That's all Coach sees. He likes hustle."

Everyone hates Brattle, the wanna-be coach, the power freak. Him and his whistle. He likes to make the kids do push-ups for any real or imagined infraction. The boys call him the Wattle because he's older and the slack skin on his throat quivers when he blows his whistle.

"Don't give him an opening," Oliver says. "Don't call attention to yourself. The Wattle will make your life miserable."

Nobody messes with Oliver, not even Brattle. At 230 pounds, he's your basic gentle giant. He stops fights by tackling both opponents, one in each arm, and taking them to the ground. Oliver isn't fast, but he's deft with that first-baseman's glove. And when he gets hold of a pitch, he doesn't need speed. He can walk around the bases.

Walking up Mission toward the BART station, Oliver talks to Bennie about the other guys on the team.

"Mason's the one," Oliver says. "He runs the Rams. He's more than just the catcher."

So Bennie begins to watch him. It's true. Mason calls the pitches. He huddles with Coach on the batting order—who should hit, who should sit, who should pitch. Coach always seems to agree.

Before each game, Mason meets with the infielders so they know the plan for pitching against each particular player. Whether he can pull it off or not, of course, depends on the pitcher. Most of the young hurlers can't do what Mason wants them to do. They're still battling themselves.

But Ken can follow Mason's instructions. He can hit his spots. He can vary speeds and occasionally he can break off a decent curve.

The whole team is better behind Ken. When he's on the mound, they know what to expect and how to position themselves. Ken can hit too. He has two home runs on the first game against Westlake. No wonder he's everybody's baby.

Bennie, on the other hand, is a mixed blessing for the Rams. He's all energy, all enthusiasm. He's all over the field. Sometimes that's good. Sometimes it isn't.

When the players run wind sprints, Bennie is so far in front there's no one near him.

He's the one who grabs so many grounders during infield practice that the second baseman, shortstop and first baseman just sit down on the ground and watch. Oliver's amused, but he also cautions his friend.

"You're showing us up," he says. "Take it a little easy. Sometimes, at least."

It isn't that Bennie is trying to make anyone else look bad. He's simply a better infielder than most high school students. And he isn't used to having other people on the field. He makes errors because he forgets where he belongs and goes after somebody else's ball.

"Cmon, Bennie," Ken complains. "You're not the only guy on the field."

In one game against South City, Bennie is playing second when the batter hits a looper toward shallow right. Bennie takes off after it, running full speed with his back to the plate, and crashes straight into Edge, the rightfielder. They both go down in a heap. The ball dribbles into right field and, by the time anyone gets to it, the winning run crosses the plate.

"I ought to beat your head in," Edge says, as he picks himself up and shakes out his arms and legs.

It's pretty ugly and then Sarah Ann in the stands starts screaming.

"Hot dog, hot dog, hot dog! Beanie is a hot dog."

She keeps repeating it like a chant and waving her hot dog at the dugout. A few other people copy her.

Coach is livid afterwards. He sits Bennie down in front of the whole team and he draws a wedge on the chalkboard that covers behind and on the first-base side of second base.

"This is your job," he says and then BAP, slams the chalk down on the third-base side of second.

"This is not."

BAP. Right field.

"This is most definitely not," he shouts. "Got it?"

"Yessir," Bennie answers.

Then there's the game when Bennie hits a ball in the gap and races head down so hard he forgets there's anyone else on base. He runs into Ken at third. They're both out and the Rams are out of the inning.

As they walk off the field, Ken shoves Bennie to the ground.

"Get out of here, you screw-up," he mutters.

Bennie clambers to his feet and shoves Ken, who's walking away. Ken stumbles, but manages to keep his feet. He turns back and charges, just as Oliver grabs his arms and two other players grab Bennie.

For the last couple years, Bennie hasn't spent any time with Ray. He walks by the custodian's trailer, up on the hill behind the school, on his way to the bus stop. He sees Ray from time and time and they wave at each other.

One day late in his freshman year, Bennie is surprised to see a baseball rolling down the hill. He catches it, of course, and looks up to see Ray standing there.

"Thought that would get your attention," he smiles. "Bring it back up, will you?"

He's sitting on his picnic table, his stiff leg straight in front of him, when Bennie gets to the trailer.

"Got a new job," he says, grinning, as Bennie flips the ball to him.

"Super," Bennie says, wondering why Ray's telling him. "Are you leaving the school?"

"Oh, no, it's a second job," Ray beams. "I'm an usher at AT&T."

"Hey, that will be great." Bennie remembers Ray talked about how he wished he could afford to go to more Giants games.

Ray laughs. "It's a dream job. If you even call it work. I'll be at every home game, except the day games during the workweek. All the night and weekend games. I started 28 innings ago."

He pushes himself to his feet and shows Bennie his official ballpark badge.

"But that's not why I asked you to come up here. How'd you like a job?"

"Me? Doing what?"

"They're looking for a kid to load up the food, clean up, stuff like that. You won't get to see the games 'cause you'll be working inside the stadium under the seats. But you'll be there. And they'll pay you for it."

Is Bennie interested? Way interested??

"What do I do?"

"I'll put in the word for you."

So Bennie has a rare stroke of luck. A friendship resumes and Giants baseball consumes his summer.

AT&T Park. The hidden elevators, the back stairs, the short-cut under the playing field. The doors and tunnels only the staff knows about.

A Big League stadium is like a castle. There are hundreds of rooms in the huge structure. Battlements where you can look unseen on the entire playing field. Places where the workers rest and re-fuel before they put 50 pounds of coffee on their backs and climb up and down the stadium stairs. Secret passageways, like ones behind the Jumbotron scoreboard or under the outfield arcade.

What a place to explore!

Bennie is supposed to report for work three hours before game time. That means he's got to be there at 10 a.m. for a day game (except for school days), 4 p.m. for a night game. He's usually there hours before that.

Long before the gates are open to the public, he watches the Giants stretch and warm up, learning their personalities, fascinated by everything they do. He watches as the players run through their fielding drills.

Bennie is two small eyes and one big Giants hat, leaning on the first row railing, keeping out of the way of the sweepers and cleaners combing the stands. Few people notice him, taking it all in.

He's at the indoor cage when the players have their individual sessions with the hitting coach, Dewey Dunston. He played for 15 years, mostly for the Giants, and ended his career with a .305 average. He likes to start the guys out with some swings, followed by some swings, and then some swings.

"Turn your hips," he calls to player after player. "Use your legs."

Bennie's on the other side of the glass, trying to stay out of sight, going through the motions himself.

Dewey teaches the Giants to be poised for each pitch—to hold their bats the same way, to have their weight balanced, their grips solid.

"No, no no," he corrects a young player. "Get up on your toes. Put your feet a little wider. Get a solid stance."

He works with each player on specific problems. Sometimes he talks about the way they hold their bats. Sometimes it's chasing bad pitches. Sometimes losing their center when they reach for a pitch.

"You're in control," Dewey insisted. "You don't have to swing. Don't let the pitcher fool you."

He teaches the batters (and Bennie) how to think like a pitcher. What would he throw in a particular situation—depending on the number of men on base, the number of outs, the score of the game, the way the hitter swung in his other at-bats during this game, the pitcher's personal history with this batter?

Dewey exhorts the Giants over and over: "Head in the game. Keep your head in the game."

"Head in the game," Bennie says to himself as he carries and stacks boxes, as he clears and cleans behind the scenes at AT&T. "Keep your head in the game."

He learns the names of the attendants, the sweeper-uppers, the groundskeepers. He learns how to taste a blade of grass to find out whether the field is fast or slow. He sees how they prepare the base paths, smooth the pitcher's mound and lay down the chalk base-lines and boxes. He watches the care they take with the team logos.

He gets to know the batboy and sometimes he helps him out. That gets him into the locker room occasionally. None of the famous Big League players pay any attention to the short kid carrying towels or removing dirty uniforms, but he's paying attention to them. He observes the way they tape their ankles, the way they oil their gloves, the way they gather themselves for the competition.

Bennie works hard, unloading heavy boxes full of food—peanuts, jars of chili sauce, hot dogs, syrup for soft drinks. When the park is full of hungry fans, it's hectic and demanding labor.

But about halfway through the game, he's finished with his work. He scores a free meal from one of his friends. Then he drifts upstairs to Ray's section, where his old friend points him to one of the great box seats left open when season ticket holders didn't show up.

A terrific setup.

One night Ray shows Bennie to a front-row box and he discovers that Unk is seated next to him. He's so delighted that he doesn't notice at first how sad Unk looks.

"What's the matter?" he asks.

Unk tells him he is moving back to Japan to take care of his sick mother.

"I came tonight to say goodbye," he says. "I leave in the morning."

Bennie is heartbroken. He hasn't seen a lot of Unk since he started high school, but they greet each other on neighborhood streets and sometimes they talk briefly about a Giants game. Unk always notices something that Bennie overlooked.

"I should've spent more time with you," Bennie says. "I'll miss you."

"You have great spirit, Mr. Bennie. You have something special. You will find it."

"What do you mean?"

Unk smiles gently.

"You must find it for yourself."

Bennie's schedule keeps him hopping most of the summer. When he isn't working, he's working out.

Up the hill. Down the hill. Up the hill. Down the hill. Every morning, as he goes through the old man's routine, Bennie remembers what Unk said. He remembers his odd smile and wonders what he meant.

Now that he can afford it, Bennie goes to the batting cages with Ken and Jeffrey a couple times. He wants to share all he'd learned at AT&T, but they aren't interested.

"You're getting to be crazed, Bennie," Ken says, making a monster movie crazy face.

It hasn't been the same with Ken since their fight.

Bennie wants the other boys to play pepper with him, but they aren't interested.

"No fun with three people," Ken says.

"Yeah, you need at least five," Jeffrey agrees.

Bennie wants the boys to join him on the hill. Out of the question.

"It's an illness, Bennie," Jeffrey says. "This constant need of yours to punish yourself."

"Remember when we'd spend all afternoon just reading comic books?" Ken asks.

"There wasn't anything else to do."

"That's the point. Not having anything to do."

Bennie snorts. He has plenty to do. Baseball in the morning. Baseball in the evenings. Work in between.

Another night he doesn't show up at Ray's section by the middle of the game. Ray's concerned because he knows the boy is at the park. After the game, he finds him in the corner of a club level storeroom, fast asleep.

"You missed a good one," he tells Bennie as he wakes him for the ride home. "The Giants won in extra innings."

Junior year. Things get harder.

Bennie has been slipping money to Ma every week, so she won't have to depend on Mike for everything. Toward the end of September, Mike sees the exchange and grabs the cash from Ma.

"That's not for you," Bennie says, stepping nose-to-nose with Mike.

"What's hers is mine, Shortstuff."

"Give it back!"

Bennie knocks the wad of bills out of Mike's hand. It falls to the floor.

"Get out of here! Out!" Mike is incensed. "You don't pay your share, you're on the street."

Ma puts both hands to her face. "Ohhh."

Bennie kneels to pick up the scattered bills. Then he goes to the kitchen and grabs a large garbage bag. He crosses to the dining room and stuffs his clothes in the bag.

"Oh, Bennie, no ... " Ma whines.

She follows him outside. Bennie stops and hugs her.

"Don't worry. I'll be fine."

He slips the bills into her dress pocket.

Sniffling, Ma watches her son walk away, the bulging garbage bag bumping against his butt. She reaches in her pocket for a tissue to wipe her nose and transfers the money to her bra before she turns back to the apartment.

Bennie shuffles through the foggy night. Where can he go?

Ken is out. They're just not that close any more.

Ray? No room in that tiny trailer.

He has no real friends at school, now that Oliver has graduated. He sits at McDee's for a couple hours, thinking things through, until a cop eyes him suspiciously and the boy moves back into the mist.

Turns out there's room at Oliver's place, after all. One corner in the men's bedroom is unoccupied during the night shift. Bennie takes it gratefully.

The move brings Bennie back into Oliver's orbit. He's a positive influence on Bennie.

Oliver is going to the local junior college, Skyline. "Paving the way," he tells his younger friend. He says the schoolwork is a lot more difficult than at DC.

Bennie is struggling with his studies. Tired and bored, he actually falls asleep in class twice. He's failing math because he hasn't bothered to turn in his homework.

"One D and they kick you off the team up here," Oliver informs him.

"Really?"

They hit the books together in the evenings, crowded into the corner of the kitchen. Sometimes Bennie meets Oliver at the Skyline library, where they can claim a study room for themselves.

Oliver plays first base for the Skyline squad, which he claims is " a lot better than DC." During the off-season, he stays in baseball shape by taking part in a special program designed by Coach Wolfton. He coaxes the coach into letting Bennie join a half-dozen college kids.

Wolfton believes that the key to good hitting is to develop the special muscles and reflexes required by batting. He has the boys do a series of unusual exercises.

■ He underhands two balls at the same time and tells the batter which one to hit while they're in the air.

- He puts the boys and their bats in the school pool, where they practice swinging in waist-deep water. He has them swing from both sides. It builds strength and steadiness.
- He puts the boys in the dance studio, surrounded by full-length mirrors on three sides. They critique each other's swings, again switch-hitting.

The drills influence Bennie's brand of batting. They each play a part in his personal style. But nothing makes as much difference as the lonely hours he spends at the practice wall.

As the rains begin in November and the special Skyline program ends, Bennie goes back to the pocket park every chance he gets. He hops off the BART two stops early on his way back to Oliver's apartment. He spends the last half-hour before it's too dark to play. He's there on the weekends too, rain or shine.

It's a solitary study for Bennie. It's too wet for tennis and the net is down, so he stands at half-court. He throws the ball up and bunts it at the practice wall.

He tries out different ways to strike the ball—straight on, cutting down, cutting up, slicing toward the right, toward the left, chopping straight down. Like a scientist in his chilly outdoor lab, he puts a chalk mark on the wall where the ball hits it. He jots down the kind of swing and where it goes on his pocket notepad.

He charts his results. He begins to understand how to make the ball spin. If a pitcher can do it, why not a batter? He discovers how to make the ball jump to the left or right after it hits the ground. A few times, he manages to make it bite and bounce backward.

The ball rolls back to him. It stops at his feet like a trained puppy. Bennie stands there, his bat by his side, trying to get his head around that.

All those countless hours, all those taunts from his so-called friends—all coming due. He's on the verge of a unique batting style, something entirely his own. He's trying to do something that nobody else has ever done before, to control the way a batted ball behaves *after* it hits the ground.

Suppose that's what Unk was talking about?

The batting cages are closed during the wet weather, so Bennie never has a chance to try his new technique against pitched balls until the Rams start practice in late January.

Live pitching is a lot different, especially with high school hurlers who have trouble with their control. Bennie has all he can do to hit the balls thrown at him at all.

But he keeps at it. One hand high on the barrel of the bat, he attacks the pitches. He chops. He stabs. He jabs. He slices. He cuts. He does everything he can to duplicate the effects he was getting at the practice wall.

He misses a lot of pitches. That's not a problem, not in January. Most of the guys are really rusty. They haven't swung a bat all winter and they're seldom getting good wood on the ball.

The problem is that the pitches aren't missing Bennie. He keeps getting hit. He's so intent on trying his strokes on the ball that he forgets to get out of the way. He gives new meaning to the term *battered*.

"Hey, Bruno," Coach Cortes says. "The idea is to hit the ball. Not the other way around."

"Coach, I've got this thing I'm working on."

"That's fine, son, but you need to learn to hit the normal way right now," Cortes says.

"Let me show you, Coach."

"Some other time, son."

"Do what the Coach tells you, Bennie," Brattle warns, "or you'll wind up on the bench."

He makes the boy do 50 push-ups.

Ken takes Bennie's batting trials as a personal affront. He feels that Bennie's unusual strokes distract him.

"C'mon, Bennie," he complains. "We're trying to play some serious baseball here."

"That's what I'm doing, Ken."

"No you're not, Bennie. You're goofing off. You're playing some grade-school games."

Ken demands perfection. He demands it of himself and from everyone else. But the young pitcher is often less than faultless. A throw goes wild. A curve doesn't break. A corner is missed. It happens to the best major league pitchers every game.

When it happens to Ken, he gets mad. When he gets mad, he gets worse. He makes more mistakes and that makes him madder.

Bennie starts taking normal swings when the coaches are watching. He remembers what he learned from the Giants hitting sessions. He stays balanced and he gets his share of hits.

But he goes back to his personal approach whenever he can.

If the coach is looking away, he grabs the barrel with one hand and turns that bat sideways or up and down. He chunks a bunt, he gets hit or he strikes out. He hardly ever gets on base during his batting investigations.

As the season commences, Bennie and Ken are the anchors of the team. Jeffrey makes the squad, but he stays on the bench most of the time, a back-up outfielder.

Ken is the number one pitcher that Coach Cortes always longed for. He wins eight games. Not bad for a 30-game season. But he's terrible when he loses. He has hissy fits, complete with shouts and curses and kicks. He mopes around for days, re-living each run scored off him.

Bennie has a stellar year in the field. He's an outstanding second baseman. The Rams lead the league in double plays, thanks to his acrobatic pivots and leaps.

He learns to lose himself in the flow of the game. The grass, the leather, the ball smelling like dirt, like sweat, sweet and somehow right. The rhythms. Pounding his fist into his glove. The pitcher's pawing at the mound. The batter taking his swings. It's the way baseball breathes.

The runner edges off the base. The first baseman extends his glove. The shortstop tips onto his toes. The catcher flashes his signs.

Everybody take a deep breath … throw the ball!!

Bennie also likes to run. His legs are strong and he can run faster than most high school catchers can gun. He steals all the time.

But he costs Ken a win on an away game in South City when he's caught trying to take third.

"Can't you just stay put?" Ken demands.

"I was trying to get into scoring position," Bennie answers.

"You were showing off," Ken rages.

Bennie walks away. It's that or a full-on fight. Things can't get much worse between them.

Cortes doesn't take sides. He knows that Bennie is reckless, yet he steals too many bases to stop his running.

Bennie is less successful at the plate. He bats .256, far below his personal expectations.

He keeps working on special strokes. He tries them out once or twice each game. Little by little, he begins to get the feel for live pitching. He occasionally manages an infield hit, where the ball seems to scoot sideways, frustrating the fielders.

He gets on base just enough so that the coach ignores his individual style of batting most of the time. Not all the time.

"Gimme 50, Bruno."

Brattle points to the ground. Push-up territory. Bennie bunted with two strikes and the ball went foul. A strikeout.

For the most part, Bennie gets away with it. He's simply too good in the field to bench.

One day in an away game, Bennie's bat cracks but doesn't split. He has no replacement and he prefers the familiar feel of his own bat, so he decides to keep using it. *Clonk! clonk!*—he taps the knob on the ground. The bat buzzes in his fingers when he hits a foul ball. Not surprisingly, he decides to bunt.

When he strikes the ball, the bat deadens it—*tonk!* The ball lands about 15 feet up the third base line and stops … dead. The third baseman stumbles and runs past the ball. By the time he recovers, Bennie is standing on first.

"Did you see that?" he asks after the game. "What if you could do that on purpose?"

Ken shakes his head. "It's cheating," he says.

"Why?"

"It's not right. You tampered with the bat."

"No, I didn't. You did it."

"I did it?"

"Isn't it the pitcher who cracks a bat?"

"Whatever causes it, the bat's not normal. It could fly apart. It endangers the fielders."

Bennie makes the sound and gesture of an explosion.

"I'm serious. You're crossing the line," Ken says.

"What's your problem?"

"You just can't leave it alone, can you? You've always got to get an angle. You can't just play the game."

"I am playing the game," Bennie says.

"No, you're not. You're trying to change the game. You're trying to tweak this, tweak that, always looking for some little …"

"That is my game."

8

SKIP CAN'T SLEEP the night before the playoff.

He's tired, worn down. He didn't plan on having to manage another game. For the first time, he feels his age. He knows he needs to be sharp tomorrow. He needs his rest, but as soon as he shuts his eyes, he sees another instance where something went wrong. A guy dropped the ball as he transferred it from his glove. A man didn't run fast enough. A throw bounced in the dirt …

He drifts off and then startles awake, another misplay on his mind. He keeps going over the mistakes over the last two weeks.

They shouldn't even have to play tomorrow. They should already be the champs. They sure haven't played that way for the last few games, though. How can the Bears turn it around?

What happens if Robbie gets hit hard? How do we replace Johnnie? Will the kid be ready to play?

What do we have to do to win? What do we have to do?

Coach can't sleep.

He thinks about the player revolt and how angry it made him. He took it personally. It felt like a direct challenge to his authority. Is that the way it was really meant?

How does he feel about how it turned out? Skip was brutal. When he finally moved, he ended it just like that. It was almost over anyway. It was dying of its own weight. The guys were getting sloppy. They wanted someone to take back the control.

Everybody's following orders now, but the spark seems to be missing. They're not getting the big hits. Bruno's not getting many hits at all.

Will the rook even be able to play? Can we win without him? What are we going to do about him?

Those bunts, those twisties. They drive Coach crazy. They drive fielders crazy too, he's got to admit. It can be pretty amusing. It can change an inning, having the other team falling all over each other. The fans get into it.

Coach shifts position, trying to get comfortable in the lounger where he naps through the late news. He turns off the TV, but he's too weary to drag himself to bed. He lies there worrying.

Now Pedro's gone. The Bears could have used his big bat tomorrow, but they don't need his strikeouts. Johnnie's gone. That really stings. There's nobody else on the team who can play third base the way Jett does. There's nobody with his energy. Sometimes it drives the entire squad.

Michael Thurston will take Johnnie's place. Called up from Double A a day ago. Decent range, the few chances he's had at third. He'll have to do.

A single game. Not a series like the Big Leagues, but one lonely game. Anything can happen. Somebody's bad day, a strange bounce, a freak play. One game. Only one. It's scary.

Bennie can't sleep.

His ankle is throbbing. He probably tried to do too much today, but he had to find out if Smitty's special shoe was going to work.

He doesn't want to take any pain pills, even though Smitty got him a prescription. He wants to be alert tomorrow. He won't be as agile as usual and he certainly won't have the speed he normally counts on, but he needs his fast reactions.

I can handle defense if I cheat in a little bit, he thinks. I can do it. I'll get by, if I'm careful.

He's worried about how he'll do at the plate. He can keep his weight on his back foot, keep it off that sore left ankle. What does that mean? He'll have to get it out of the infield. He can't run out any bunts.

Unless he can confuse the Quakes. Unless he can make 'em run into each other or something like that. But Coach would never put up with that ... or would he?

We've got to find a way.

Ken can't sleep.

He didn't get to his room until 2:30. He hates that team bus. He was too tired to sleep after all that jouncing. He took a shower and then he lay down, too wired to shut down. Now it's 5 a.m. and light is leaking past the hotel drapes.

He only faced Bennie in that one game about a month ago. Otherwise, he hasn't seen him since their falling out nearly three years ago. A lot has happened since then.

He went to college for three semesters. He dropped out when he got an offer from the Quakes last spring. He moved into the starting rotation in the middle of the year. He worked hard. He earned the start tomorrow.

Ken is the Quakes best pitcher now. He's a star in his own right —a 20-year-old with a big burner and a monster hook.

He knows how popular Bennie is with his hometown fans. They love his trick hits. Ken vows he will not fall victim to Bennie's quirky game. It's not going to happen to him. He's been working on a special pitch, a change-up with an unusual backspin. He's certain that Bennie's never seen anything like it before.

Ken heard about the player revolt. He heard Bennie was hurt. Will he even play?

Assume he does, so how can he get him out? What he can throw to him, pitch-by-pitch? When should he use the special pitch?

Coach is there early, of course. No surprise there. It's nearly two and the game doesn't start until 7:15. He's not alone.

He was hoping he'd have a few minutes by himself in the empty ballpark. He should have known. Workers are crawling all over. They're putting in extra seating in the outfield, big metal bleachers. They're putting up red, white and blue bunting on all the fences.

There's a big banner on the scoreboard in center: *2012 California League Championship.*

He's seen this field a hundred times—no, make that a thousand—but today it looks different. Somehow it seems smaller today, the fences shorter, the whole place shabbier. The decorations don't disguise it.

When you're here every day, you don't notice anymore. You don't see the chipped paint in the stands, the stains on the concrete walkways. It doesn't register how rundown Van Vranken Stadium has become.

Groundskeepers are sprucing up the infield. They're going over it inch-by-inch. They pull any weeds. They pat down the grass, packing down uneven spots, making sure the surface is smooth. They lay new chalk marks.

Coach is looking for any advantage, same as always, but he's looking for something else too. It's hard to express what it is—good omens, perhaps, some positive energy? Whatever it is, it's not there. All he can sense is tension, a feeling that something is about to happen, something significant.

Like a winner-take-all game.

Not only is this the big game, but it's also the final contest of the season. It's the last time these guys will set foot on a baseball field for months. And it's the last time this team takes the field together. People will come and go by next spring. It gives everything a special charge. Like a holiday or birthday. Or a funeral.

For Rancho Cucamonga, Coach hopes.

He's glad the Bears won the coin toss, that they'll play at home. It helps to have your own fans cheering you on.

Up in the booth, Cubby is working with the sound gear and talking to Goldilocks. They probably plan some special cheers for tonight.

Camera crews are setting up along the foul lines. There will be a lot more media coverage than usual tonight. Coach sees station call letters from Sacramento and Riverside. In the right field corner, a straw hat pushed back on his head, Van Vranken is taping an interview with an ESPN reporter.

"We'll make toast out of this team," he brags. "They better be *quaking* in their boots."

There's a little bite in the air and the breeze is already blowing. It will be flat-out cold after dark. Coach isn't complaining. There's been years when it snowed in September in Grass Valley.

The cold makes the field play harder. Balls travel a little faster, bounce a little higher. It hurts more if you catch it with something other than your glove. It should be to the Bears' advantage against a Southern California team.

Football weather, Coach thinks. The trees around the park are turning. The kids are back in school. That's one reason why they decided to play a night game, so the kids and their folks could attend.

The other reason is to give the Quakes a few hours of rest. They didn't get in until real late last night after the long bus ride up I-5. Rancho Cucamonga players should be real road-weary. Too bad. That's another advantage, Coach thinks, as he looses a largish yawn.

He gradually becomes aware of another sound, a slamming, a rhythmic impact, repeated every few seconds. It's coming from behind the clubhouse. He walks over to the corner to see what it is.

Bennie is at the wall. He throws the ball. He catches the ball. He throws the ball. He catches the ball. He glides from side to side, testing that special shoe with the high, reinforced top that Smitty built him, testing the ankle. He's in a rhythm.

Wham! Shuffle, shuffle. Snag, set and throw.

Wham! Shuffle, shuffle. Snag, set and throw.

He relaxes into it. His breathing deepens. His body loosens, limbers. He feels better than he has in days. The anxiety starts to seep away.

Wham! Shuffle, shuffle. Snag, set and throw.

In his mind, he replays the last few games. He remembers how he dived for a grounder to the right of the mound, cutting Richie off. He probably should have let the first baseman take it. He was overplaying. He won't be able to do that this game.

Wham! Shuffle, shuffle. Snag, set and throw.

He checks the ankle. Doing OK. Maybe this is going to work, after all.

He looks up and there's Coach, standing and watching him. Bennie smiles—tentatively. He's uncertain about how Coach feels.

Coach is about to say something, but Skip comes around the corner and interrupts.

"Look, you two. I want to talk."

Two hours until game time.

Most of the guys are in the locker room under the stands. Some are finishing the sandwiches that Smitty laid out for the team. Some have their stuff partway packed. They've got plans to get out of town for the off-season right after the game. Guys are giving things away.

"You want some glove oil?" Frankie has three cans left over from the season.

"What you readin', Devo?" Abe Emery is looking over the short-stop's shoulder. "That a comic book? Lemme see."

Robbie and T.J. review the Quakes hitting chart, talking about each batter and how they want to pitch to him.

"You remember" stories bounce around the room, punctuated by joking and fist bumps. You'd never know the title was on the line.

The vibes are great, especially when you consider the Bears have lost five of their last six games and the Quakes have won four of five. The guys are loose and full of fun. Coach feels good about his decision. The team meeting seems to have made a real difference.

Outside, Goldi and a few friends—all of them very female —are on the sidelines out by right field, working on some steps.

Skip and Coach run the guys through a few stretching drills and they take a long, leisurely BP. The bats hitting the ball, the thwack when a guy gets hold of one—all the sounds are bright and brittle in the chilled air. The grass smells good. The dirt does too.

Coach starts to feel a little better, a little more hopeful.

The stands are filling up. Little kids are running around all over the place, chasing any balls that get past the fielders. They're leaning over the railings as the Bears take their cuts. It's like a Big League field before a game.

Coach hangs around behind the cage, like always.

"The Quakes are hot," he tells T.J.

"Robbie seems ready. He's got 'em all working," the catcher answers.

Robbie Creamer, the Bears starter, is an old warhorse. By the end of the season, he's tired. He plays tired. He lives tired. Living on the road half the time takes its toll on you when you get into your thirties.

He's off by himself on the bench an hour before the game. It's so solo, being a starter. No one comes near him. Let him collect himself or whatever. It'll be that way during the game too. When the Bears are up, Robbie's in his own world. Nobody looks at him.

The Quakes are cocky. They act like they're princes on parade or something. They throw the ball around the infield real brisk and business-like. They look sharp and focused to Coach. But their shortstop is a little lame. He's favoring his left knee. And their bullpen is worn out. Those relievers had to work hard for that final win Sunday.

On a big game like this, there's always a game within the game. This time the story is probably Bruno and Sato. The two of them grew up together in Daly City, according to the Sacramento Bee. The Bee has a reporter covering the contest. There's someone from a Daly City paper here too.

Before they take the field, Skip gathers the players one more time in the clubhouse. Instead of standing up and beating his chest—which is what most managers do at a time like this—he sits down on one of the benches by the lockers. Most of the players are standing.

"Been an interesting year," Skip says.

That brings some chuckles and a couple outright laughs. A locker door slams.

"One more to go," he says and then he stops and thinks about it for a moment. He eyes every man in the room. He doesn't try to rev everybody up. He stretches out the moment.

"Do yourself some good today," he says quietly.

Then he gets up and leads the Bears onto the field. The players are a little subdued, but they're determined. And they're together as a team.

The stands are jammed, even in the outfield. Music is blaring from the big speakers and people are dancing in their seats. The fans holler and cheer when the Bears are introduced. A few wave homemade signs:

"Go Bears!"

"Quakes Suck!"

"Marry me, Bennie."

Across the field, the Rancho Cucamonga boys come out to the applause of about 60 diehard Quakes boosters, who took a bus from Southern California for the game. They all look a little wrinkled. Nine hours on the road will do that to you.

Bennie spots the Satos. Mrs. Sato gives him a quick grin and a waist-level wave as he files into the dugout.

T.J. and Bruce Benbow, the Quakes captain, turn in the line-up cards to the home plate umpire:

VISITOR: Rancho Cucamonga Quakes

LINEUP

Nate Burton	LF
Matteo Navas	2B
Bruce Benbow, captain	1B
Jorge Castillo	RF
Jack Hannagan	3B
Ron Wong	CF
Memo Covacha	C
Donnie Dale	SS
Ken Sato	P
Darcy Evans	Manager

HOME: Sierra Bears

LINEUP

Devon Highsmith	SS
Eddie Briseño	CF
Juan Murillo	RF
T.J. Thatcher, captain	C
Winston Rizzo	LF
Frankie Gates	2B
Carlos Ramos	1B
Michael Thurston	3B
Robbie Creamer	P
Skip Becker	Manager

The shadows are getting long and it's definitely nippy as the Bears take the field. Frankie starts the game at second base. Bennie is on the bench.

It's not a good beginning. Robbie is on the mound for the first time since his big win last Friday. He gives up a double on the second pitch. The Quakes leftfielder, Nate Burton, advances to third on a ground-out to the right side from second baseman Matteo Navas.

The Quakes are an Angels farm team and, like their parent club, they're a balanced squad with powerful hitting. Bruce Benbow, their first baseman, hit 32 homers this year. Jack Hannagan at third base hit 28. Rightfielder Jorge Castillo hit fourth and had a .310 batting average. The three of them are a handful, coming as a cluster in the Rancho Cucamonga lineup.

Robbie strikes out Benbow with a nasty change-up. He walks Castillo in a long at-bat that goes to a 3-2 count and lasts nine pitches. Hannagan swings over a change-up and then blasts the second pitch to the deepest part of the park. Eddie makes it exciting, but he manages to get there and make the catch.

The Bears get out of the inning, but the Quakes are shaking them. They still seem hot from their huge weekend win over the Empire. They don't score, but they're at the door. They're pounding.

Twenty-two pitches. Skip won't look his pitcher in the eye when he walks past him into the dugout.

What's worse is the bottom of the first. People say the Angels will call Sato up next season. He's that good. The Bears only faced him the one time he easily defeated them. He's in complete command tonight. The Bears go down without so much as a growl. Three up and three down. Juan strikes out for the final out on the ninth pitch of the inning.

The fans are too excited to get down about one bad inning, especially when it's early and there's no score. But Coach is worried.

In the top of the second, Robbie throws a wicked curve to Ron Wong, the Quakes centerfielder, who hits a dribbler toward second. Frankie is there in plenty of time, but he boots it. A man on first with no outs. Bennie never would have muffed that play.

But Robbie seems to regain his composure. So much of this game is mental. He gets the next batter, catcher Memo Covacha, to hit into a double play. Donnie Dale, the Quakes shortstop, hits a comebacker to the mound for an easy third out.

The Bears come alive in the bottom of the inning. T.J. leads off and puts up a tremendous fight. He makes Sato throw a dozen pitches before he slaps a grounder toward the hole. Dale makes a diving stop, pops up and throws over the first baseman's head. T.J. takes second on the play.

Coach is dancing up and down the sidelines, clapping his hands. "Great hustle," he shouts. "Attaway, T.J."

Winston comes to the plate and Coach signals for him to hit it on the ground to the right side.

Cap nose chin cap chin nose cap elbow.

Winnie does it and T.J. advances to third with one out.

The next batter is a surprise to the crowd. When it's first announced, Frankie is in the on-deck circle. He smirks and fist-bumps his replacement on his way back to the dugout.

"Now batting for second baseman Frankie Gates: Ben-nie Bru-no!"

Cubby, the PA announcer, stretches out the name, leaning on each syllable. The crowd responds with a roar.

There's no hitch in his step as he walks to the plate. Smitty's shoe is doing its job. And it didn't hurt—it didn't hurt at all—to miss the first two innings of defense. Skip's plan is working well.

Bennie takes a couple vicious practice swings and then pulls one hand high on the bat. The fans applaud.

"Bennie Ball. Bennie Ball," they call.

The Quakes infielders look at each other, then in unison check their dugout for signals from Darcy Evans, their manager. They creep in cautiously.

Coach signals to hit away: *Cap chin ear chin cap nose cap nose.* Clap, Clap.

Bennie watches him closely. Ken thinks it's a stunt. He figures something's wrong or they wouldn't have waited to put him in the game.

He throws one directly at his former friend's bad foot.

Bennie hops out of the way and manages to land on his right foot, holding his tender left foot off the dirt. He settles carefully back into the batter's box and checks Coach, who repeats the same sign.

Cap chin ear chin cap nose cap nose. Clap, Clap.

Bennie's hand slides up the bat. As the corner fielders charge, he drops his hand and swings hard at Sato's next pitch. He drives it to center, a perfect sacrifice fly. When Wong hauls it in, Coach windmills his arm. T.J. takes off from third and scores.

Even though Devon grounds out, the Bears are ahead. Coach pats the rook on the shoulder as they go back to the field.

	1	2	3	4	5	6	7	8	9
Quakes	0	0							
Bears	0	1							

The Quakes pitcher leads off the top of the third. You'd think it would be an easy out, but Sato has a reputation for being pretty good with the bat. Robbie grooves one, a curve that breaks right across the plate, and the rookie pitcher tees off. He hits a high drive toward the gap in right field. He takes off and makes it all the way to third before Juan manages to get the ball back to the infield.

Robbie looks grim. The Quakes leftfielder hit a double off him the last time he was up, but Burton doesn't have a chance this time. Robbie throws him four balls off the plate. Nothing even close.

"I hope that was on purpose," Coach tells Skip. They're both hanging on the rail, each with one foot on the lip of the dugout.

"You and me both."

Skip is suffering. It's what managers do. He leans against the rail like it's a church pew and he's praying.

"It's only the third inning," he says, glancing at his scorecard. The Bears bullpen is thin. They only have two relievers who can pitch—Sonny Young and Gene Wood. Skip could go to Mattie in a pinch. He started three days ago and lost, but he's a warrior.

"C'mon, c'mon," Skip mutters.

He peeks over the rail, as Robbie issues his second straight walk to the Quakes second baseman.

Bases loaded. Nobody out. Not a good position for the Bears to be in. Rancho Cucamonga's heavy hitters are coming up.

Skip goes out to the mound and T.J. trots out to meet him there.

"How do you feel?" Skip asks Robbie.

"I'm fine," Robbie says. Robbie always says that. He'd say he's fine if his arm was one pitch from falling off.

Skip looks him in the eye. Robbie doesn't flinch.

"OK," Skip says. "Be careful of this guy. Don't walk him." And he trots off the field.

Benbow steps into the box. The Quakes first baseman struck out his first time up, but he carries a gaudy .321 average into the playoff.

Skip signals for the infield to back up a few steps in hopes of a double play ball.

"Let's go, Robbie," Michael yells from third.

"Let's go," Devon echoes.

Fists pound the gloves like drums, a little baseball backbeat.

Coach claps his hands. The crowd noise gets a little louder.

Robbie gets ahead with a nasty curve ball that breaks in on Benbow's hands. Then Benbow swings at a low pitch and sends a screamer at Bennie, who fields it cleanly and throws to home, forcing out Sato. T.J. relays to first in time for the double play.

Robbie takes off his hat and wipes his forehead with his arm.

Two outs, runners at second and third, the Quakes clean-up hitter coming up. The Bears can still get out of the inning without a run scoring against them.

Robbie reaches back. He sends a challenge fastball, perfectly placed on the outside corner, but Castillo smacks a liner to left.

Two runs score. Winston's throw from left field nails Castillo as he tries to stretch his hit into a double. The inning is over, but the damage is done. The Quakes are ahead 2-1.

Devon gestures with both arms to Goldilocks and her cheerleaders.

"C'mon, Goldi. Get the crowd into it."

The girls are happy to oblige. They prance and kick in front of the stands.

"Let's go, Bears! Let's go, Bears! Let's go, Bears!"

The PA announcer gets into it too, turning the mic on the crowd and amplifying their cheers.

"LET'S GO BEARS! LET'S GO BEARS!"

But all they can manage is a two-out single before Eddie fouls out and strands Devon at first.

The Bears get another good inning from Robbie in the fourth. Three up and three down.

Moving through the batting order for the second time in a close contest, both teams are still feeling each other out. It's still anybody's game.

Juan struck out his first time at bat. This time he's very choosy. He makes Sato throw strikes. He takes the count to 3-2 before he lofts a short fly that falls in front of the centerfielder. T.J. works a walk, sending Juan to second. Winston strikes out.

Bennie comes up with runners on first and second and one out. Quakes infielders move in, but only slightly, reasoning that Bennie can't run well enough to play smallball.

Skip gives the nod and Coach signals: *Chin ear chin ear chin nose cap nose.* Clap, Clap. That's the take sign. Coach wants to make sure everyone is in synch.

Bennie lets the first pitch go by without moving. Juan and T.J. stay put. The Quakes infielders come up on their toes, but they don't move in.

The rook looks back toward third.

Chest ear chin ear chin nose cap chin. Clap, Clap. Put it down. Then Coach touches his chest. With his right hand.

Sato throws a wicked inside pitch. Bennie sucks in his gut and brings one hand higher. Then he yanks his bat straight down, cutting at the ball and sending it dribbling toward first.

The fans leap to their feet, screaming.

The ball bounces just inside the chalk. Benbow charges, but the ball bites and hops abruptly toward the pitcher's mound. As Benbow tries to change direction, his feet go out from under him and he falls onto his side. He reaches for the ball and the Quakes catcher, also in pursuit, trips over his outstretched arm and goes down too.

Sato steps carefully over both bodies and picks up the ball. Bennie has plenty of time to get to first. Juan and T.J. advance easily to second and third, running at contact because they knew the ball would go right.

"Ben-nie! Ben-nie!" The fans call his name.

Ken is agitated. It happened after all. Bennie got him with one of his trick hits. He kicks the dirt behind the mound, trying to tamp his temper.

"OK, folks," The PA announcer bellows. "Time for the Bears to take that home field advantage."

Bases loaded. The fans are cheering. It's a big chance for the Bears. Most of the players are on their feet, pushing against the rail, eager for their turn at bat.

But they don't get it done. Sato regains control—of himself and the game. He gets Carlos to ground into a double play. Bennie is the lead runner and he only makes it halfway to second.

	1	2	3	4	5	6	7	8	9
Quakes	0	0	2	0					
Bears	0	1	0	0					

The Bears go back onto the field and Coach walks back to the dugout, disappointed that they didn't score but gratified that the new signals seem to be working. What a relief. When you only tell the guys at the meeting before the game, it's a gamble that they'll remember.

He's pleased Bennie got on base. The surprise factor worked. The Quakes never expected a twisty hit with that bum foot of his.

If the Bears were surprised when Skip told them, they hid it pretty well. There were some looks across the clubhouse, but nobody said anything. Everybody seemed ready for Coach and Bennie to patch things up for the sake of the team.

Now everybody is on the same page. Bruno gets to hit his crazy twisties—sometimes, but not all the time—and runners know where the ball is heading when he does. But he also hits the sac fly when Coach tells him to. He obeys the take sign.

At bat and on the bases, the Bears offense is back in Coach's capable hands. The way it should be, he thinks, as he takes his place at the railing. He claps his hands. Got to stay warm. Got to keep the guys fired up.

"Let's go! C'mon, let's get 'em!" he shouts, as the Quakes short-stop strides to the plate.

Coach admits, at least to himself, that he could've let his feelings about the rook get in front of his clear thinking, Maybe just a little. Skip convinced him it's a good call to bring back smallball.

Neither team makes much progress in the fifth. Sato gets on for the Quakes, but he's stranded at first.

In the bottom of the inning, Robbie is pulled for a pinch-hitter, Richie Dean. He strokes a single to right and Devon draws a walk, but the Bears can't get anyone home. They threaten again, but cannot break through.

Sato records his seventh strikeout. He's the biggest reason the Bears are behind. In the dugout between innings, he changes into a long-sleeved tee under his uniform shirt. He huddles in the corner in a warm-up jacket with a muffler around his neck.

The top of the sixth is short and not sweet. Sonny Young is on the mound. Skip figures that the lefthander will turn around some of the Quakes, making them bat from the other side, and just generally make it more difficult for the others. The strategy works for Benbow and Castillo, the number three and four hitters. They hit soft fly balls, both to Winston in left.

But Hannagan turns on one of Sonny's offerings and sends it over the centerfield wall. No matter that Wong flies out too, it's 3-1 Quakes.

The crowd gets uncomfortably quiet, but the cheerleaders begin some leg kicks. The fans join the chant as T.J. settles into the batter's box in the bottom of the sixth.

"Bears! Bears! Bring it to 'em, Bears!"

But it doesn't do any good. Sato is as sharp as ever, chalking up strikeout number eight with a nasty slider down and away. T.J. slams his bat back into the rack.

Winston battles Sato, fouling off vicious curves and cutters. On the seventh pitch, Sato misses and Rizzo knocks one into left.

Bennie comes up with a man on. The crowd starts to clap. A few fans start to chant:

"Bennie Ball! Bennie Ball! Bennie Ball!"

The Quakes infielders move into a special two-tier defense. The first and third baseman charge, while the shortstop and second baseman stay back.

The hubbub in the stands fades out after the first pitch. It starts outside and swings across the plate for the first strike. Bennie nods at Sato, as if to say, great pitch.

Chin ear cap chin ear nose cap nose. Clap, clap. Coach calls for a hit to the outfield.

Bennie moves his hand up on the bat, causing the infielders to charge. At the last moment, he brings both hands down, but he doesn't swing at a fastball low and outside. The ump calls strike two.

Bennie doesn't believe it. He looks back, but he doesn't say anything.

Coach repeats his sign: *Chin ear cap chin ear nose cap nose.* Clap, clap.

Bennie waggles his bat back and forth a few times. The guys in the dugout lean forward. The fans stir again.

Ken decides this is the time. He positions his fingers for the special pitch that he's been saving for his former friend. He's never used it in a game before.

The pitch comes right down the middle and then dips at the last second. The spin is all wrong, backwards.

Bennie lurches at it and nicks the ball into the catcher's mitt. Strike three.

The crowd groans. Bennie only struck out a dozen times during the entire season. He could always be counted on to put his bat on the ball.

Sato won that one with three amazing pitches. Bennie looks grim as he takes the long walk back to the dugout with a decided limp.

Carlos goes down in two pitches, a well-hit line drive caught by Donnie Dale at short.

	1	2	3	4	5	6	7	8	9
Quakes	0	0	2	0	0	1			
Bears	0	1	0	0	0	0			

Young comes out for his second inning. He's calm and assured. He records three quick outs from the Quakes.

The Bears are eager to bat in the bottom of the seventh, but Sato is eager to pitch to them too. He's throwing like he's inside the hitters' heads. He keeps shaking off Covacha. He wants to call his own game.

Devon ekes out a two-out, nine-pitch walk, but Eddie follows with a strikeout on four pitches. Number nine for Sato. Another easy inning for the Quakes hurler.

Skip puts in Mattie Fleming for the eighth. He threw two innings three days ago in his final regular season game against the Storm. Even though he got shelled, he's been the Bears' steadiest man on the mound over the whole season.

The top of the Quakes order is due up. Burton, Navas and Benbow are all excellent hitters. T.J. confers with the new pitcher on the mound.

Mattie is the oldest Bear, aside from Skip and Coach. He's been a fixture in the California League for more than 15 years. He gets by on guile, not on power. His fastball is so-so. His curve is occasional. But he can put his sinker anywhere he wants to, anytime he wants to.

He feeds Burton a steady diet of them, frustrating the brawny leftfielder, who sends a tame grounder to Devon at short for the first out.

Navas stands in. The second baseman has one walk to show for his efforts for the night. On the first offering from Mattie, he slams a towering fly to right. It goes over Juan's head and bounces into the new outfield bleachers. A ground-rule double.

Then Benbow, the opposing captain. He takes a ball and swings at Mattie's second pitch, hitting a rising line drive toward first. Carlos goes up for it, but the ball deflects off his glove. He falls on his rear at the end of his jump, which takes him totally out of the play.

But Bennie is backing up the first baseman. He makes an adjustment when the ball comes off Carlos' glove. He lunges, comes up with the ball and hops to his feet. Benbow rounds first and heads for second, but Bennie launches his body at him and tags him out three steps off first base. Both men go tumbling onto the grass with the impact.

The crowd goes ballistic. The brilliant defensive play saved another Quakes run.

Benbow glares at Bennie as the two men pick themselves up. Bennie pauses, leaning on his right knee. Skip and Smitty come out to see if their second baseman can continue.

The fans are on their feet. Even the owner, Van Vranken, is cheering. Applause fills the stadium as Bennie gingerly puts weight on his left foot and limps back to his defensive position.

The next Quakes batter is almost a comedown. Castillo is a dangerous hitter. He scored the first two Quakes runs with a single in the third. But Mattie gets him on a long fly down the right-field line, just foul.

The outfielders start to run in, then see what's going on and slow to an unhurried walk. Like Bennie, who can't run off, not any longer. His painful, deliberate journey to the dugout sets the pace for the rest of the Bears.

Everyone in the place is on his feet and applauding.

"Ben-nie! Ben-nie! Ben-nie!"

But on the other side is Sato. The fans tend to overlook what's happening in the Quakes dugout. Sato is leading his team to the brink of victory with a beautiful game pitched under playoff pressure.

So far, he's given up six hits in seven innings, all singles, and he's walked three. He's only allowed a single run.

The Bears are all at the rail, as Juan takes his stance in the box.

Chin cap elbow cap chin ear chin nose.

Coach signals for him to hit away.

Instead, Sato hits him. Juan doesn't try very hard to get out of the way and an inside pitch plunks his thigh. He takes his base.

A rare mistake by the Quakes pitcher. It irks him. Sato smirks at Juan, but then recovers by getting T.J. to hit a grounder to third. Juan is forced out at second and T.J. barely beats the throw to first.

Two runs down, Winston takes his place in the batter's box. He's one for three with a strikeout and a single. He needs to get on track.

The crowd is getting raucous. Spurred on by Goldilocks and her girls, the fans are competing with each other to see which section can shout the loudest. They're doing this stand-up-sit-down thing, a wave moving from section to section.

Winston is waggling his bat back and forth and scuffing his feet like a pony. Sato wastes one in the dirt, but Covacha blocks it.

The Quakes catcher calls for an inside pitch, knee-high. Winston swats at it ineffectively. He can't quiet himself down and get a good swing against Sato.

Most minor league hurlers would be out of the game by now, but Sato shows no apparent strain as he nears the 100-pitch mark. He seems as strong as ever.

He throws a slider. Winnie lunges at it and slices a one-hopper deep into the hole at short. Dale gets to it, but he has to hurry his throw. The ball skids past Benbow at first.

The Bears have two men on with one out as Bennie hobbles to the plate.

The Quakes call a conference at the mound to decide how they're going to play defensively. Bennie takes a few cuts and watches the proceedings.

The Quakes edge in from first and third again. The shortstop moves over, so he can cover third, if needed. The second baseman cheats a little toward first.

Chin, nose, chin, ear, elbow, belt, elbow, ear.

Coach signals for a hit-and-run. It's a risky play with two men on, but the Bears need to score at least one run this inning.

The fans chant: "Ben-nie! Ben-nie! Ben-nie!"

Sato winds up and throws. Winnie takes off from first. T.J. breaks from second. He's a fireplug, big and slow like most catchers, but he runs as hard as he can.

Bennie slides one hand up on the bat, which forces the infielders to charge. At the last instant, he slides his top hand down again and swings hard. He's trying to bloop the ball over the head of Hannagan, the charging third baseman.

But the bat shatters and pieces go flying. One shard heads for Hannagan, who puts up his arm to deflect it, causing him to miss the ball, which rolls past him and stops dead. Another piece of the bat hits Sato in the shin.

By the time the Quakes shortstop gets to the ball, it's too late to get anybody out. T.J. comes all the way around to score. The Bears have runners on first and second with only one out.

Sato is steamed. The wood from the bat tore his pants leg and blood is oozing from the wound. The Quakes trainer goes to the mound to see if his pitcher is OK.

"Check his bat!" Sato shouts to the umpire standing between first and second, pointing at Bennie. "Check his bat!"

The batboy picks up the pieces and gives them to the ump, who examines the broken bat while the trainer puts a bandage on Sato's leg and rolls the pitcher's pants leg down.

"What am I looking for?" the ump asks.

"He shattered it on purpose," Sato says. "He used a cracked bat."

"Not true," Bennie says, standing on first. "There was nothing wrong with the bat." He's definitely favoring his left foot, putting all his weight on the other foot.

The fans boo. They don't like the delay.

"I can't tell anything from these pieces," the ump says.

"He did it on purpose," Sato insists.

"I didn't," Bennie says.

"Boooooo!"

"I've seen him do that before," Sato says. "I tell you, it was planned."

The ump shakes his head and motions for the game to resume.

"Play ball," he says. "Get on with it."

Sato is still annoyed, but he takes a few warm-up tosses to show the trainer and the Quakes manager that he is all right. As they go back to the dugout and Carlos steps up to the plate, Sato glares and points at Bennie at first base.

"Cheater," he hisses.

"It was your pitch," Bennie answers. "You broke that bat."

"Boooo!" The fans start again.

"Let's go," the umpire insists.

Sitting in his squat, Covacha gestures with both hands down toward the dirt, telling Sato to calm down.

Coach sees how irritated Sato is and decides to take advantage. He signs to Winston at second:

Chin, belt, chin, belt, cap, belt, nose, chin. Steal. Do it now.

The Quakes don't expect it. On the first pitch, Winnie gets a great break. Covacha catches Sato's pitch, an off-speed ball to the inside, and fires to third. But Hanagan isn't near the bag and Winnie is safe.

The fans come to their feet again. The noise is huge. It's like a living thing.

Is Sato finally losing it? The Quakes pitcher is upset, but he tries to hide it. He walks around the mound. He adjusts his cap. He gets back onto the rubber and throws to first.

Bennie isn't going anywhere. He nods at Coach. Great call.

One out. A fly ball brings home a run. The fans can taste the tie. They want it.

Benbow walks the ball back to his pitcher, trying to settle him down.

Sato stands on the hill again and shakes off the catcher's signal. Then he takes a deep breath, rares back and chucks a slider in the dirt. This one gets by Covacha.

Winnie scores the tying run and Bennie gimps over to second.

The ballpark is a din. A celebration. It's one loud, brute yell.

Sato shuts them up. He gets Carlos to hit a soft liner to first. Bennie has to stay where he is at second. Sato realizes that Skip has no more pinchhitters on the bench, so he walks Michael on purpose.

Mattie comes up. Skip has no one to bat for him. He only had two extra batters on the bench and he used them early. Bennie subbed for Frankie in the second and Richie Dean batted for Robbie Creamer in the fifth.

Mattie fans on three pitches for the third out.

But the Bears are excited as they traipse out of the dugout and back onto the field for the ninth. It's a new game. The players seem to catch a second wind. They run to their places on their field, trading fist bumps and slaps with each other.

	1	2	3	4	5	6	7	8	9
Quakes	0	0	2	0	0	1	0	0	
Bears	0	1	0	0	0	0	0	2	

Knotted up in the ninth. The next run could be the winner.

Mattie goes out to the mound for his second inning of work. He had an impressive eighth inning, thanks in large part to Bennie's brilliant defense. Can he keep it up in the ninth?

Hannagan is the first batter. He homered in the third Quakes run. Mattie throws a high one. Ball one.

Every pitch is crucial now, this late in the game. Every swing brings a gasp from the fans, every miss a groan.

Mattie throws a low one. Ball two.

T.J. stands and starts toward the mound. Mattie waves him back. He takes off his hat and combs his hair with his hand. He tucks in his shirt.

Then he gets back on the hill and throws two more balls. Hannagan trots down to first.

T.J. walks the ball back to his pitcher.

"Slow down," he says. "Nobody's got noplace else to go."

Skip gets Wood up in the bullpen.

Wong's turn. He's 0 for 2. He was safe on an error in the first. He checks third for the sign and waits for the pitch.

Mattie throws two balls. Wong backs out of the box, swings his bat a couple times and steps back in.

Mattie goes through his routine again—the hat, the shirt, the rosin bag. This is a big pitch.

It comes in too good to be true, right over the plate. Wong practically swings out of his shoes. There is an intake of breath from the fans, as the ball sails into the sky. It's hard enough to break the tie. It's long enough. It's … foul.

A sigh of relief from the crowd. A howl of disappointment from the Quakes dugout.

Hannagan was all the way around second by the time the ball came down. He goes back to first.

Mattie's next pitch is just outside. The one after that is low. He doesn't really want to get near Wong's bat.

The fans groan as Wong takes his base with the second walk in a row. Hannagan moves to second.

Skip makes his move. He goes to the mound and takes the ball from Mattie, ignoring the pitcher's pained expression. He gives the ball to Gene Wood. He doesn't usually bring his closer in when the game is tied, but this isn't a usual game. This is the championship.

Wood has three pitches, all fast balls, but he varies speeds and he has pinpoint control. The batter knows what's coming, but he doesn't know when or where. Gene earned 18 saves for the Bears.

Two on and nobody out. The Quakes catcher comes to the plate. He's had a horrible night offensively, 0 for 3 and hit into a double play, but he's called an excellent game. He's asked for the right pitches at the right time.

Wood throws a ball under his chin. Covacha hurls himself backward. He gets up, dusting off his pants, scowling at the pitcher.

Wood's second offering is in almost the same place. Both teams come to the dugout railing, ready to run onto the field if there's a general brawl.

Covacha picks himself up a second time and gets his helmet and bat. He holds up one hand to tell his teammates not to charge the field. He takes his time getting back together and settling in.

Wood's next pitch is over the outside corner. Covacha reaches for it, a little awkward because Wood has him back on his heels, and nubs a grounder right at Bennie at second. He throws to third and barely gets the force out on Hannagan.

One out, runners at first and second.

Dale steps into the box and takes a few practice swings. He's 0 for 3.

On the first pitch, he lines one right back at the pitcher. Wood is just finishing his follow-through. The crowd gasps. Gene instinctively throws his glove in front of his face. He knocks down the ball, but the ball knocks him down, as well. He scrambles to his feet and looks around. By that time, all three runners are safe.

The fans are buzzing. Skip and the trainer start out of the dugout, but Wood gestures that he's all right.

The bases are loaded as Sato comes up. He's had a triple and a double in his first three times up. He makes a big show about kicking out holes for his feet in the batter's box. He takes off his batting gloves and pulls them on again. He adjusts his helmet.

Wood waits patiently. He's used to these shenanigans. He knows Sato is trying to bug him and he's not about to let that happen. He's a veteran. He's seen just about every trick there is to psych out the pitcher.

Wood fires a pellet past Sato on the inside corner. Strike one.

T.J. comes out of his crouch as he returns the ball to the mound. "That's the way, Gene baby. That's the way."

"One more like that," Bennie calls. "One more."

The second pitch is also inside, but this one is too high. 1-1.

Sato steps out and adjusts his equipment again. Wood fusses with the rosin bag. He checks all three runners, as he climbs back onto the hill.

He throws another ball, high and outside, his fastest speed. Sato watches it go by. 2-1.

The next pitch is in almost the same spot, but it's considerably slower. Sato whacks at it and the ball skims under Wood's glove. The pitcher brushes the ball, but he can't catch it.

But Devon is right there. He grabs the ball, trots to second himself because Bennie is moving so slowly, and then tosses to first for an easy double play.

No score. Inning over. The ballpark explodes.

Coach is a little surprised to see Sato go back to the mound. He faced seven batters in the eighth. He's thrown over 110 pitches.

He's been real tough. There's been a lot of men on base, but only three scored. That last inning was hard on him, but he only gave up one hit and that was Bennie's broken-bat single.

None of that matters now as the game goes to the bottom of the ninth. All that matters is the present—the next pitch, the next swing, the next instant.

The PA crackles with a corny "fight" song. Goldilocks leads her girls in a few leg kicks.

Fifth time through the batting order. Both teams know each other well, the Quakes and the Bears.

Devon stands in. He's been on base three times, two of them walks. The Bears need number four. They need one more.

"Let's go, Devo," Coach yells from third. "Get us started."

Chin, nose, cap, nose, chin,, arm, chest, leg. Clap, clap. He signs for him to hit it a ton.

Devon takes a huge uppercut on the first offering from Sato. He's trying to end the game with one swing, trying to be the hero.

Sato sees it and plays to it. His second pitch is barely off the plate and Devon takes another major cut. The ball traces a massive arc across the sky and lands 30 feet foul. Just what Sato wanted— strike two.

Shouldn't have given Devon that sign, Coach thinks. The boy needs to get hold of himself. He claps a few times to get the batter's attention.

"Devon," he yells. "Hey, Devon!"

When he finally turns back toward him, Coach makes the push-ing-down motion with both hands. He's trying to tell him to tone it down, think small.

But Devon isn't listening. The third strike is another swing from the heels. It sails over Sato's slider, which falls down and away.

Sato turns his back and walks around the mound, rubbing up the ball. Even this late in the game, he doesn't want to show up the batter. He doesn't want to give the Bears any reason to get any more keyed up than they already are.

Eddie is 0-4 with three strikeouts. Sato has been a total puzzle to him all day long. You'd never know that he's been out there for nearly 120 pitches, the way the Quakes pitcher is throwing.

A ball, outside. Eddie is choked up on the bat. He's thinking small.

Another ball, also outside, and then a strike. 2-1.

Cap, chest, cap, chin, leg, chin, nose, wrist. Clap, clap. Take another one.

On the fourth pitch, Sato misses high. Again, Eddie holds up.

3-1. Sato needs to get the next pitch over and Eddie knows it. But he loses his patience. Like Devon before him, Eddie takes a big swing at Sato's lovely curve.

The ball goes to Dale at short, who throws to first for the out.

Two down. Juan is up. The Bears number three hitter, suppos-edly their best. He's been on base three times—a couple singles and hit by a pitch. He stands outside the box, taking a few extra swings and staring at the pitcher. Holding one hand up to call time out, he carefully positions himself at the plate.

Sato throws the fast ball, but it misses inside, pushing Juan a couple stagger-steps back. So much for that special footing.

Scowling, he re-sets himself and swings his bat a few times. He goes after Sato's next pitch and sends a sizzler toward third. Hannagan gets in front of it. It looks like a routine throw to first. But the ball takes a strange bounce and hops over the third base-man's glove and into left field. Juan pulls up at first.

Sato is peeved, but that kind of thing happens all the time in baseball. He has to forget it.

T.J. gets a chance to end it. He steps to the plate and looks back for a sign. Coach gives him a fake one.

Leg, cap, wrist, chin, cap, chin, wrist, chin. Clap, clap. Do whatever.

"Get it done, T.J.," he shouts.

The rest of the guys are at the railing, willing their catcher and team captain to win the game. Skip looks 107 years old. Juan takes a small, safe lead off first.

Sato shakes off Covacha. That's the first time he's done that this inning. He fires a fast ball over the inside corner for a strike.

T.J. backs out of the box, shaking his head.

Coach hand-talks him again. *Cap, chest, elbow, chest, nose, chest, cap, nose.* Clap, clap.

As instructed, T.J. lets the next pitch go by, a curve right over the plate. 0-2.

On the next pitch, he swings hard and hits a clean single to right. Juan only makes it to second, as Castillo returns the ball to the infield.

Two on, two out, as Winston moves to the batter's box. Sato doesn't even check his dugout to see what his manager wants. He wants to work to the next batter, the one with the bum foot, the one from his childhood. It's almost like it was meant to be.

He walks Winston on four pitches, loading the bases.

The fans come to their feet and start calling his name again.

"Bennie! Bennie! Bennie!"

Skip knows he ought to pull Bruno out of the game, but he doesn't have anybody to replace him. He wouldn't pull him if he could. The kid is all beat up and lame, but he's also an inspiration.

The fans start to stomp on the floor of the bleachers.

"Bennie Ball!" *(Stomp! Stomp!)*

"Bennie Ball!" *(Stomp! Stomp!)*

Bennie has two hits in three official at bats. He's been amazing in the field. He's in major pain and, although the night is clear and very cold at this point, he's sweating profusely.

Sato uses a full windup. He doesn't pitch from the stretch. He doesn't need to shave those seconds. None of the runners is going to risk making the third out by trying to steal now.

Sato throws an inside fastball, missing the plate, watching how Bennie gets out of the way, how he jackknifes and stumbles a little. Bennie struggles back into position and swings his bat.

He bats right, which means his front foot is the sore one. He puts weight on it at the end of his swing. Or when he's off-balance. Ken wants to make him use that left foot.

Will he fall for that killer backspin again? Not yet, Ken decides. He collects himself and throws a sinker, trying to make Bennie lean over the plate.

Bennie takes a ball. Now it's 2-0.

Sato turns his back on the plate. He wipes his mouth and his nose. Bennie is swinging his bat. The fans are on their feet, applauding and stamping. Goldie and the girls are kicking near the sideline.

"Bennie Ball!" *(Stomp! Stomp!)*

"Bennie Ball!" *(Stomp! Stomp!)*

Strike. Bennie is fooled by the curve and swings early. He manages to maintain his balance.

Strike two, a fastball in the dirt, but Bennie swings over it. He's not himself. He's not crouching and getting ready for one of his signature smallball hits. He's favoring his injury.

Sato throws another wide one. Ball three. The pitcher whirls, disappointed with the call. He paces behind the mound.

Full count, 3-2, bases jammed. There's no place to put Bennie, no pitches to waste. Bennie can't let a good one go by. Something, someone has got to give.

Bennie looks back at Coach, who gives him an uncharacteristic grin. He's savoring this moment. He flaps his hands.

Cap, wrist, cap, wrist, cap, chin, cap, elbow. Clap, clap. One more time, rook.

Bennie looks out at Sato. Sato glares back at him and spits on the grass. It comes down to this, one will against another, the former friends facing each other with the season on the line.

"Bennie Ball!" *(Stomp! Stomp!)*

"Bennie Ball!" *(Stomp! Stomp!)*

Ken looks up and notices the fans huddled in the cold. Even when they're standing, they're hunched against that icy breeze. Some have their hands at their throats to hold their coats closed.

And Sato shivers. For just a second, the cold gets to him and that makes him tired, exhausted really, and that makes him angry. Stupid bus ride up that endless freeway. Stupid shattered bat.

Sato takes a deep breath and then lets it out, lets it all go. He shakes his hands to get them warm. He gathers his strength and looks at the plate.

There's Bennie, always ready, always waiting for him, pestering him, pushing him. OK. You asked for it.

"Bennie Ball!" *(Stomp! Stomp!)*

"Bennie Ball!" *(Stomp! Stomp!)*

Bennie is totally immersed in the moment. His pain is distant, unimportant to him. He can't feel the cold. He can't feel the sweat pouring across his face.

Unconsciously, he wipes his eyes. Everything is extra sharp, extra detailed. He's completely focused. It's what he learned at the wall, all those thousands of hours.

At the same time, he's aware of the huge night beyond the stadium lights, the huge quiet on the other side of those tremendous cheers. He steps out of the box. He taps into that quiet. He looks out far past the fences, past the bleachers, to the Sierra foothills. He looks in, deep inside.

"Bennie Ball!" *(Stomp! Stomp!)*

"Bennie Ball!" *(Stomp! Stomp!)*

The sounds of the crowd fade for Bennie and Ken. The pitcher finds his special grip.

Coach signals: *cap, wrist, cap, chin, leg, cap, chin, cap.* Clap, clap. Give me somethin' twisty, rook.

He pats Juan on the back and moves down the line, edging closer to home. He catches T.J.'s eye and then Winnie's.

Clap, clap. He touches the right side of his cap.

Bennie steps back in. He brings his hand high on the bat.

Ken goes into a full wind-up, ignoring the runners on base. He puts everything he has, all his anger, into his throw, his fingers pulling down at release to give the ball that terrible backward spin.

Bennie sees the movement on the ball. It falls toward his back foot. It might be out of the strike zone, but he's not going to risk it. He swings low across his shoe and lifts the bat sharply, putting a spin on Sato's spin.

The ball spurts toward the mound, wobbling slightly, and strikes Sato on a short bounce on the side of his calf.

"Ahh!"

The pitcher stumbles, but keeps his balance, facing toward first.

The ball squirts toward third, twisting erratically.

Grimacing in pain, arms churning, Bennie staggers up the line.

Sato curses and reverses, as Juan crosses the plate with the winning run. But they can still throw Bennie out.

The third baseman gets to the ball, but it's like it's alive, it's squirming, it's quivering. He can't hold on to it and it falls to the turf.

Sato snatches up the ball, gets a good grip as he twirls and throws. Bennie, hopping on his good right foot, sprawls forward and reaches for the bag.

The ball SMACKS into the first baseman's mitt.

"Safe!" the umpire shouts.

The fans go nuts.

"The Bears are the champs! The Bears are the champs!" the PA announcer shrieks.

Bennie struggles to his feet, his hands high in the air, and the other players mob him.

"Bennie Ball! Bennie Ball!"

"Bennie Ball! Bennie Ball!"

The fans are delirious.

Skip shares a glance with Coach, the can-you-believe-it look. And Coach—his stomach suddenly wonderfully at ease—slaps Skip's outstretched palm and the two of them walk toward the jubilation.

The boys lift Bennie onto their shoulders and Skip flips him the game ball.

"Here you go, young man," the manager says. "You certainly earned it tonight."

Most of the fans are still standing, hugging, cheering, applauding.

"Bennie Ball! Bennie Ball!"

"Bennie Ball! Bennie Ball!"

Bennie looks across the field to the visitors' dugout, already empty except for a single figure, just picking up his jacket and turning toward the tunnel to the clubhouse. He must have waited there to watch the Bears' celebration.

"Kenny! Kenny!"

The Quakes pitcher looks back. Rocking on his teammates' shoulders, Bennie holds the ball aloft and grins.

Sato smiles back, puts his hands together and bows to Bennie. He starts to leave.

Bennie clambers to the ground, emerging from a pile of players who are still patting his back, rubbing his head, laughing and punching each other's arms.

"Kenny! Wait up!"

He limps as fast as he's able across the infield, still so elated he can hardly feel the pain. Marching music tuned too loud distorts the stadium speakers. Fans are still milling around, leaning out of the stands, screaming with victory.

"Bennie! Bennie!"

He waves the game ball at them and hurries down the ramp to the lockers. Sato is waiting out of sight from the field.

A private moment, muted amid the clamor and blare, as Bennie catches his breath. He looks down at the game ball in his hand and then flips it to the man who had been his best boyhood friend.

"This belongs to you."

THE END

ABOUT THE AUTHOR

Bill Baynes is also a producer, director and creative director. He has been reporter for the *Miami Herald* and the Associated Press and won awards as a documentary filmmaker. Active in feature film and video production, magazine publishing, public interest marketing, and website development, he has also worked with school systems to create student-driven media campaigns.

For their help with this book, my deepest thanks to:

Donna, for her ceaseless love and support, as well as her perceptive reviews.

Jim Minter, longtime friend, publisher and editor, whose encouragement made this book a reality.

Charlotte Minter, co-publisher, friend.

M.J. Sullivan, Barry Hodgin and Matthew Schoenfeld, for repeated insightful readings.

Anne Robinson and Lee Eisler, for their patience and participation in our ongoing critique group.

SILVERBACK SAGES, PUBLISHERS

The "silverback" was originally an old gorilla, an alpha male. Lately, that word has mingled with the "silvertip" label for old grizzlies (ursus horribilus), and becoming generic, is popularly applied to old boars, rats, pit bulls, squirrels and raccoons. Today, a silverback could be any furry alpha critter surviving into old age, male or female—even a human. As for sages, there is a certain natural wisdom that comes with just surviving; it's those methods of seeing and ways of action that might possibly guide the observant young towards their own inner wisdom.

As to publishers, these days it's tough for older writers to find a publisher, even for very good books. Our mission is to publish and to keep in print the high-quality works of those new and seasoned writers who are not marketable enough for the financial thirst of contemporary publishing.

Our Upcoming Books:

In This Living Body
by M. J. Sullivan

BUNT!
by Bill Baynes

Ghost of the Great Albino Boar
by James F. Hutchinson

Shingyō
by Seihō

Visit us at: www.silverbacksages.com

Silverback Sages, Publishers, L.L.C. was licensed in Northern New Mexico in early 2011.

CPSIA information can be obtained at www.ICGtesting.com
Printed in the USA
BVOW021537280213

314358BV00004B/6/P